ANNIE OAKLE
in Double Trouble

by DORIS SCHROEDER

*An original story
featuring ANNIE OAKLEY
of the famous television series*

Illustrated by TONY SGROI

Authorized Edition

WHITMAN PUBLISHING COMPANY
RACINE, WISCONSIN

Contents

1   The Ambush

In the pleasant ranch house kitchen, Annie Oakley was spreading the square pine table with a checkered cloth. She could hear her Uncle Luke's cheerful whistle out at the barn, where he was giving the horses their breakfast oats and fresh water. But from the second floor bedroom there was nary a sound from her small brother Tagg.

Annie reached for the broom and lifted it to pound on the ceiling just under her sleepyhead's room. That was their daily signal for him to roll out of the covers and start dressing for school.

But even as she raised the broom, she remembered that there would be no school today, even though it was the middle of the week. They had no teacher at the Diablo School! The very prim and proper young lady who had taught there for the past two years had eloped suddenly with a handsome young miner who had just struck it rich up at Soapstone, the booming new gold town ten miles away.

Now Tagg and the other youngsters who lived in and around the desert town of Diablo would have a vacation till fall. Maybe longer, if the very fussy school board couldn't find a teacher who suited them by then.

That was just fine with the small fry, including young Tagg Oakley, age eleven; but it made quite a few problems for their elders. Annie had no intention of letting Tagg give up school work for all that time. Somehow, even if it took a struggle, she intended to see to it that he did some studying every day. But, as their Uncle Luke told her with a chuckle when she announced her plan, that might take some doing.

Annie was a slim seventeen, pretty in a freshly wholesome way. A little row of freckles marched across the bridge of her pert nose, and her blonde hair was caught up in two shining, short braids which were tied at the ends with saucy little bows. When she had housework and cooking to do, she wore a big starched white apron over her usual costume of riding blouse, fringed divided skirt, and decorated leather vest. She made a pleasant picture to the tall sheriff as he came in from his chores at the barn.

"Breakfast is ready, Uncle Luke!" She was stacking his plate high with well-browned flapjacks from the big iron griddle on the wood range.

"No readier than I am!" he chuckled. "I washed up at the barn so I wouldn't waste time getting down to business."

By the time he had settled in his chair and taken his napkin from its silver ring to spread across his lap, she had his plate set down in front of him and his oversized coffee cup filled. "How's this for service?" she laughed.

"Best in the world!" he smiled. Then he sobered. "Annie, honey," he told his niece solemnly, "every time I recollect the long years I lived here alone, eating my own miser'ble cooking, I get the cold shivers. Shoe-leather flapjacks, burnt beans, an' coffee as black as a claim-jumper's heart!" He sighed and shook his head. "The day you and little Tagg decided to come West here and join me was the luckiest day of my life!"

Annie smiled affectionately at him. "Not half so lucky as it was for us, Uncle Luke. We've been with you only a little over a year, but it seems like we've always lived here."

"I'm glad of that," the sheriff nodded, "because it's rightly your home, Annie, yours and Tagg's. Your mother spent some happy years here, before she married your dad and went off to be a cavalry officer's wife. She'd be pleased if she knew you two had come home."

"I reckon she knows, all right, and Dad does, too," Annie said softly, her blue eyes brimming suddenly. "I remember, right after the fever took her off, when I was seven, Dad told me he was sure she'd be waiting for all of us, somewhere up ahead. And I figure, even if it *was* way up in the Sioux country that he was killed, he found his way to her straight off."

Sheriff MacTavish's heavily lined face softened. "I don't have the least doubt of that, honey."

For a little while they sat silent, lost in thought. The food lay cooling on the sheriff's plate, while he stared unseeingly out the window across the wide desert valley. He was remembering a pretty, high-spirited girl—very much like the one who sat across from him now—who danced so gaily at her wedding in this same old ranch house, and then rode off forever with handsome young Lieutenant Jared Oakley. The empty spot that she had left in her adoring big brother's heart had never been filled till her orphaned girl and boy had come West to live with him, after the death of their gallant father, Colonel Oakley, in the Sioux uprising.

Annie moved suddenly and pointed toward the sheriff's

plate. "I do believe you don't like my cooking, after all, Uncle Luke! I think I'll throw it out to Tagg's pet pig Esmeralda!" She pretended to reach for the plate.

Sheriff Luke lifted his fork threateningly. "You lay a hand on my elegant breakfast, young woman, and I'll spear that sassy trigger finger of yours!"

They both laughed, and Luke proceeded to douse the flapjacks with butter and thick molasses, while Annie brought over the big graniteware coffeepot in readiness for the second and third cups of coffee she knew he would want.

The hallway door opened suddenly and Tagg came blinking into the sunlit kitchen. "Golly, Annie!" he said crossly. "Why didn't you call me? I'll be late for school!" He staggered over to the sink and began dipping water into the tin wash basin from the bucket.

His uncle started to speak, but Annie, eyes twinkling, laid her finger to her lips and shook her head warningly. She went about getting Tagg's breakfast ready, while he was splashing and moaning and muttering about the coldness of the water.

Suddenly he stopped, with the water running down his face, and faced Annie accusingly. "Hey! I clear forgot! No

school today! Why didn't you remind me?" He was about
as disgusted as Annie had ever seen him. "I could've slept
an' slept!" he moaned.

Annie and her uncle kept straight faces. "But think what
a nice long day you'll have now! You'll have time to study
your spelling and arithmetic!" she said innocently.

Tagg's face was getting longer by the minute. Uncle
Luke couldn't stand it. "I thought you said you'd take this
young'un prospectin' at the wash today."

Tagg brightened at once. "That's right! So you did,
Annie! You said we might find a—you know, for the—you
know!" he reminded her, grimacing mysteriously.

Annie set his milk and hotcakes in front of him. "I give
up! One of you I can battle, but when you men gang up
on me, it's just no use struggling! We'll take the day off,
like we planned. But tomorrow you study!"

"Of course, Sis!" Tagg's tone of voice indicated that
there was no question about tomorrow. But Uncle Luke,
pushing his chair away from the table, bit back a grin. The
little rascal would have some other excuse tomorrow, to get
out of studying. And, like as not, his uncle would weaken
and help him put it over!

"I'd better start for town now." Sheriff MacTavish took

his gun belt from the hook beside the back door and buckled it on. He shook his head and sighed as he checked over his heavy Colt revolver to make sure it was loaded and ready for action.

The sheriff of Diablo was a peace officer in the best sense of the title. He hated the need for violence, but having pledged himself to enforce the law, he did it to the best of his ability. If he found it necessary to use his gun, he did it. But he was proud of the fact that in all the seven years he had served as sheriff of Diablo County, he had never killed a man, except in a fair fight and in self-defense.

He was not out to make a reputation as a gun fighter, but to convince the criminal element that law and order were firmly established in his county.

Annie came over to him and spoke softly, so Tagg wouldn't hear. "Expecting trouble, Uncle Luke?"

"Nope!" he answered cheerfully. "Just making sure I'll be ready in case any starts."

"Who's in our jail now?" Annie was mildly curious.

"Nobody right now," the sheriff looked grim, "but Lofty's due back on the afternoon stage from Bonanza City, bringing some information we've been waiting a long time to get, all the way from Texas. If it turns out to be what I expect, our jail's due to have a full house, pronto!"

Annie walked to the barn with him, while Tagg finished breakfast and started making himself a giant-sized lunch to take along on the prospecting trip. If he did as much digging out at the wash as he was planning, he would have an appetite to match the sandwich!

When the sheriff was ready to ride, he told Annie, "Better keep Tagg away from town for a day or so, if you can. We may have a little trouble when we start rounding up some of the troublemakers."

Annie nodded solemnly. She was wishing she could help her uncle clean out the riffraff and gamblers that the gold strikes up at Soapstone had brought into peaceful Diablo. It was on the road to the new diggings, and many of the wilder element had taken to lingering in Diablo to "entertain" the miners on their way through. And usually to cheat them out of their gold dust or anything else of value. There had been some sad cases lately, and the decent citizens of Diablo were up in arms over it.

"I'd be glad to help," she said.

"No need, honey," her uncle assured her. "Lofty and I can handle it."

Annie was very proud of her uncle, and she knew that

his deputy, Lofty Craig, was honest and efficient. But there were some things she had learned from her father that neither of them had been trained in—like picking up a trail and tracking a fugitive.

Trailing was one of the things that the late Colonel Oakley had taught his daughter when she was very small. Later, at the frontier Army posts where he had been commanding officer, he had assigned expert Army scouts to teach her the art of reading sign in all sorts of country.

Her father had taught her to handle a rifle with sure aim, either from a galloping horse or afoot. And he had trained her to handle his heavy Army Colt .45 six-shooter, which she carried now in her gun belt whenever she rode out.

She could split a coin at ten yards with the Colt, and at a longer distance she could aim the heavy service revolver almost as accurately as her Winchester rifle.

Now, as she went back to the house, she told herself sternly, "Stop fussing! The men Uncle Luke is after are all around town. So there'll be no trailing to do! Just 'tend to your own affairs, young lady!"

Tagg was waiting at the kitchen steps when she led their two horses from the barn. He was surrounded by enough prospecting tools to outfit a party of five. It took some arguing, but she finally talked him into leaving all of it behind except an iron pan for washing gravel, a pick, and a shovel. "Fortunes have been dug up with less!" she assured him. "All you're looking for is one small nugget!"

The sun was bright on their faces as they set out for Little Dry Wash, near the north boundary of the ranch. Annie hoped there would still be some water in the wash, so Tagg could splash around in it and dig out plenty of pebbles for "panning." After the summer really set in, the wash would be quite dry on the surface, without a trace of the noisy torrent that sometimes raced along it during the winter rains. Then he would really have to dig deep if he wanted to hunt for golden pebbles.

They got to their destination about noon, and Tagg had to eat lunch in the shade of a stunted mesquite tree on the edge of the wash, before he descended to the tiny stream at the bottom.

When he finally climbed down to start panning for nuggets, Annie noticed that he was carrying an empty water bag. "Looks like you're expecting to hit a bonanza!" she teased.

Tagg nodded confidently. "Inky Wiggins, at the *Gazette*

office, told me a miner over there, right at the foot of that mountain, picked up nearly a pound of nuggets one day! I figure lots of 'em could have washed down here this winter!"

Annie kept a straight face. "That mountain" was a good forty miles away! "Sounds exciting!" she agreed. "Let's see what luck you have."

Tagg dug out a shovelful of sand and pebbles and dumped them into his iron pan. Then he held the pan under the running stream, moving his hand around and around in the bottom of the pan, stirring up the contents so that the flow of the water would carry off the sand and pebbles, little by little. If there were any flakes of gold, or even the small rounded chunks called nuggets, they would sink to the bottom of the pan, and remain after the lighter sand and pebbles had washed away.

When he had emptied the pan, she called down cheerfully, "What luck so far?"

He looked up. "Nothin'!" and sat back on his heels.

"Dig deeper! Don't give up so soon!" she advised him.

"How deep do you think I'll have to go?"

"That depends on how big the nugget is!" Annie replied. "For instance, the right size to make a real nice stickpin for Uncle Luke's surprise birthday present would be kind of deep down." She added under her breath, "If it happens to be there at all!"

"Okay!" Tagg was digging again, whistling cheerfully.

Annie heard something suddenly. It was the sound of horses' hoofs, and it came from over the hill. It seemed strange, away out here in the open country, until she remembered that this far corner of her uncle's ranch stretched to the main road between Bonanza City and Diablo, and the road was just over the hill.

The *clip-clop* of hoofs came to a sudden stop, and then everything was quiet except for the usual bird calls in the brush, and the buzzing of bees among the last few wild-flowers.

The hill wasn't very high. She thought, "I bet there's a pretty view from up there," and then, idly, "Wonder who that was just rode by." She was half tempted to climb to the top and see what she could see, but she felt too lazy and relaxed.

Then, as she glanced up again, she saw something moving in the bushes near the summit. It could be a coyote hunting food. Or it might be a mountain lion stalking her two horses!

She decided to go up and take a look.

Target and Pixie were grazing peacefully, showing no signs that they had scented danger. But that didn't mean there was no cougar around. The wily beast would circle, keeping downwind of them, if he meant to attack.

She was halfway up the hill when she saw the "lion" emerge from a tangle of mesquite and thornbush. It was a big wild turkey!

Wild turkeys were scarce now, since the country was filling with settlers, but she remembered Uncle Luke telling her how the hills used to swarm with the tasty critters. She made up her mind this one was going to make a toothsome Sunday dinner.

She checked her rifle. Next time the turkey poked his head out, she would have him. She went down on one knee and leveled her rifle toward the clump of brush into which he had disappeared. She could see the brush move.

Then, as her finger started a firm, steady pressure on the trigger, the roar of a six-shooter broke the silence. In the still air, it seemed to come from only a few yards away.

She threw herself flat on the rough ground and lay motionless, holding her breath. She hoped the rocks around her hid her from whoever had shot.

The wild turkey, unhurt, squawking with fright, and trying to fly in brief, fluttering leaps, disappeared in the rocky hillside, and she could hear it moving away noisily. But there was no second shot.

Then in the stillness, she heard new sounds. Horses running, the creaking of a wagon body, and then a shout from the other side of the hill, "Pull up there!" followed by the squealing of wooden brakes and the frightened whinnying of a horse.

A different voice shouted, "Get down with your hands up!"

It was a holdup! And judging from the time of day it was happening, it might very well be the stage from Bonanza City that had been ambushed.

She remembered suddenly that Lofty Craig was to be on that stage, bringing important papers from Texas to her uncle. Papers he needed to clean up the town!

2   Annie Lends a Hand

Now that Annie knew that the shot had been fired on the other side of the hill, probably by the ambushers, she moved out of hiding and climbed up toward the ridge of rocks on the hilltop. From there she could look down without being seen from the road.

Tagg yelled up from the wash, "Hey, Sis! What's going on?"

She stopped and signaled "Silence!" Indian fashion, the back of her hand flat against her mouth. He waved in reply and didn't shout again. But she saw him run to the foot of the hill. He was going to climb up and see for himself!

The sounds of the holdup came up to her clearly from the other side of the hill. "Everybody out and line up over there! Keep your hands up!" She could hear protesting voices, and a rough command, "Git movin'!"

She moved the rest of the way to the hilltop and peered down cautiously between two rim rocks.

Her guess had been right. It *was* the stage from Bonanza City that was being held up!

She could see only two ambushers near the stopped coach. Both were wearing tan raincoats that covered them from neck to ankle, and concealed any of their other clothes that might have been easy for the victims to remember and report. They also had their plain-colored neckerchiefs drawn up across their features, and wide-brimmed hats pulled down across their eyes.

One of the men was quite tall and the other was short and heavy-set. That much she could make out, even from a distance.

Two men passengers had already been lined up alongside the road, and a third was being marched over to join them, by the taller of the bandits. The six-shooter in the tall man's hand prodded the angry, stumbling victim along.

None of the three passengers looked prosperous. She had seen dozens of traveling salesmen in better clothing. The poor fellows were probably hopeful prospectors, coming to the latest gold strike up there at Soapstone to find their fortune. She wondered what the ambushers would get from *them*.

Then she saw Lofty Craig step slowly out of the coach with his hands up. The deputy was talking angrily to the heavy-set bandit, who was waving a gun in Lofty's face with a very threatening motion. She hoped Lofty wouldn't do anything foolhardy. She was relieved when he moved over to join the other passengers after the hold-up man had taken his gun.

The taller bandit waved him into line, and then turned away to motion old Tim Kelly, the driver, to join the others.

"Now!" Annie aimed her rifle toward the ground at the tall man's feet. A shot would throw him off guard, and Lofty would have a chance to jump him. But as her finger tightened on the trigger, she saw something that made her hold her fire.

Another passenger was getting out of the stagecoach. It was a young woman, slim and well-dressed in dark traveling clothes. She held back, clutching her handbag with both hands and staring terrified at the man who was urging her to get out.

Annie was glad she hadn't pulled the trigger. It would have been sure to start a gun fight. And the young woman might have been wounded or killed in the crossfire.

The squatty bandit grabbed the young woman's arm and hurried her faltering steps toward the other passengers. She seemed to be so frightened that at any moment she might collapse.

"It's a lady!" Tagg's voice was so close to her ear that Annie jumped. She hadn't heard him come up.

"Sh-h-h-h!" she warned. "Keep down out of sight!"

But Tagg had to take another peek. "Hey!" he whispered excitedly. "They got Lofty, too!"

Annie nodded and kept her eyes on the group below.

"They won't get much from Lofty!" Tagg went on in a stage whisper. "I heard him telling Uncle Luke he needed two dollars on next month's salary or he couldn't take his girl to the dance Saturday night!"

"Thought I told you not to listen to private conversations!" she whispered over her shoulder as sternly as she could manage. But she couldn't help smiling. Lofty was quite a favorite with the young ladies of Diablo. She could just imagine what a blow it would be to him to miss taking one to a dance.

Now the two masked men were starting to rob their victims, one by one. They took a gold watch and chain from the first man, in spite of his pleading. His wallet followed, but a quick inspection showed it to be almost empty.

The second man proved to have a fatter wallet. The shorter bandit extracted the cash and bills from it, and handed them back to his partner, who followed close behind along the line-up, holding a canvas bag for the loot. He dropped the money into it and held it ready for the next contribution.

The young woman was next in line. As the squat bandit moved up in front of her, she clutched her handbag and seemed to be begging him not to take it.

Annie's trigger finger itched as she saw the fellow grab the purse roughly from the girl's hands and toss it over his shoulder to his partner coming behind him.

The tall bandit caught it and opened it. The young woman seemed to be making a desperate effort to persuade him to hand it back to her. She finally tried to reach for it, but he pulled it out of her reach quickly.

She watched despairingly as he opened the bag and drew out a small roll of bills. He seemed uncertain whether to keep it, and showed it to his partner. But the heavy-set bandit gestured impatiently to him to drop it into the bag, and the tall man obeyed.

The shorter bandit moved on to the next passenger, and the tall man, with what looked to Annie, from a distance, like a polite bow, handed back the bag to the lady, and moved on after his partner.

The young woman stared after him, and her hand went up to her throat as if something had suddenly startled her.

Annie whispered to Tagg, "I wish I was down there! He'd lose his elegant manners fast!"

"Maybe she likes them!" Tagg grinned. "She's still staring after him!"

"Scared half to death probably, the poor thing!" Annie said grimly. "Tagg, I'm going to break up their little ambush if I can get down there without being noticed!"

She stood up out of range of the people in the road below and looked all around her keenly. Then she told Tagg, "I think I have it figured out! You can give me a hand."

"Sure, Annie!"

"I've got to get down to the road where I can come around behind those two gunslingers," she explained. "My best chance to do it is to get down over there, on that side of the hill."

"But that's where the hill was cut away for the road to

go through!" Tagg objected. "You'd have to drop the last ten or fifteen feet!"

Annie shook her head. "I can handle the drop all right, if they don't hear me landing!" She smiled at him. "And that's where you're going to come in! Think you can help me?"

Tagg was willing to do anything Annie said. "Sure, Sis!" he agreed cheerfully. "What do I do?"

"I'll go around the shoulder of the hill there and start down. When you hear me whistle like this—" she gave a low trill and a liquid mockingbird call "—give this chunk of rock in front of you a hard shove with your foot and send it rolling down the hill." She pointed to a jagged hunk of granite that lay loosely on the rimrock. "Then *duck!* And stay down!"

She started moving away, keeping back from the skyline, and soon disappeared around the corner of the hill. Tagg watched her go, and then sat down and braced his back against a boulder, with his foot set against the loose granite chunk.

He could hear voices in the road, and longed to look over and see what was going on, but he'd had his orders so he just sat tight and waited.

Then Annie's signal whistle came softly. Tagg gave the piece of rock a mighty push with his foot.

It moved forward and swayed a moment on the edge of the rimrock. Then it toppled over and started bounding down the hill, making a loud crash every time it hit.

By the time the rock was halfway to the road, it had started quite a little landslide, and a noisy one.

Tagg wanted more than ever to poke his head over the edge and watch; but Annie had given him orders to stay down, so that's what he did, crouching behind the rimrock.

It was a good thing he had followed orders. A bullet from below smashed into the face of the very rock he was hiding behind and ricocheted high into the air, dropping a shower of small sharp fragments of granite on him.

Then he heard an angry voice yelling below, "Quit wastin' lead, Bill! There's nobody up there. It was jist a loose rock that let go of itself! You wanta start a big slide, jarrin' that rimrock?"

The other man's answer was drowned in the noise of the sliding, bouncing rocks and loose pebbles.

Around on the other side of the hill, Annie grinned as she heard the exchange. It was working out the way she had hoped it would.

She poised on the edge of the hillside cut, held her rifle high above her head with both hands, and made the long jump down into a patch of soft sand at the side of the road. She was a little shaken by the jump, but she had learned how to relax in falling, so she was on her feet the next moment. And her rifle hadn't so much as one grain of sand in its barrel to clog it.

She moved swiftly around the corner of the hill, rifle cocked and ready. She was still fifty feet away when she saw that the two ambushers were now robbing Lofty.

The deputy didn't see her, because he was not directly facing her. If any of the other passengers did, they had sense enough not to show any signs that would alert the two robbers. She moved up, foot by foot, stealthily.

Lofty was angrily warning the pair, but she heard the shorter bandit laugh and saw him poke his gun into Lofty's stomach threateningly. Then Lofty drew out his wallet. The robber tossed it over his shoulder to the tall man, who caught it, took out the one bill he found there, showed it to his partner, and dropped it into the bag with a flourish. Annie heard them laugh, and saw Lofty's fists double up and his face get red. They were having fun at his expense. It was plain he didn't like it.

Annie hoped Lofty wouldn't lose his temper and do anything rash, with two six-shooters ready to cut him down. But he put his hands up again and stood quietly waiting for them to go on to Tim Kelly, the driver, next to him.

Instead of moving on, the heavy-set bandit ripped open Lofty's tightly buttoned coat and reached into the inner pocket. He brought out a heavy manila envelope, long and thickly filled. He glanced at it, and then Annie saw him wave it toward his partner and exclaim, "I got it!"

Lofty started to lower his hands, and Annie heard him speak sharply. "Better not take that, mister! It's Government property!"

The short bandit laughed, and struck Lofty across the face with the heavy envelope. Annie couldn't hear what he said, because the young woman passenger gave a little scream just then and covered her face with her hands.

The tall bandit seemed startled by the scream, and turned his head to look back at her. It was at exactly that moment that his partner handed the heavy envelope over his shoulder to him, without looking to see if he was ready to take it. The envelope fell to the ground between them.

The short man heard it fall and turned to see why.

The moment he took his eyes off Lofty, the young deputy lunged at him, and gripped his gun hand to wrest the six-shooter from him.

The deputy's attack took the masked man by surprise, and he almost let go of the gun. Then he recovered and fought hard to keep it. Lofty wrestled him to the ground and they rolled over in the deep dust, battling for the weapon.

It had all happened so fast that the taller man had been caught by surprise. Now he hastily snatched up the envelope and backed away, drawing his gun, and watching for a chance to aim at Lofty.

But before he could level the gun, a bullet from Annie's rifle smashed it from his hand, and broke it to pieces.

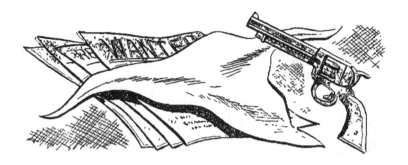

Before the ambusher could recover from the shock of having his six-shooter smashed out of his hand by Annie's rifle bullet, she was moving in quickly toward him, keeping her rifle trained on him. "Reach, mister!" she called out.

At the top of the hill above them, Tagg stood up suddenly and waved his hat. "Yi-i-i!" he yelled. "Good aim, Sis!"

The masked man had been starting to raise his hands When he saw Annie answer her brother's shout with a quick, worried look up toward the hilltop, he wheeled suddenly and started running toward the heavy brush across the road.

"Quick, Miss Annie!" It was old Tim Kelly, the stage driver. He had been wounded in the arm by the bandits' first shot, but he was still full of fight. "You can stop him!"

Annie raised her rifle to her shoulder. She decided to chance a shot into the ground well ahead of him with the hope that it might scare him into stopping.

She aimed carefully. But just as her finger started to press the trigger, she heard the lady passenger exclaim hysterically, almost in her ear, "I think I'm going to faint!" Then she toppled over against Annie, knocking the rifle off its aim and grabbing at the barrel to save herself from falling.

Annie had no chance to pull her finger free of the trigger, and the bullet exploded into the ground a few feet ahead of them. The young lady gave a faint shriek, and slumped to the ground at Annie's feet.

For one horrified moment, Annie thought the bullet might have struck the girl, and she hastily laid aside the rifle to kneel beside her. She saw right away that the girl had only fainted.

Lofty and the heavy-set ambusher were still fighting for possession of the gun, but Lofty seemed to be winning. Annie looked after the tall man, and saw him just disappearing into the thick undergrowth beyond which their horses must be hidden. If she moved fast, she might be able to overtake him before he could escape with the loot.

One last look at Lofty showed the tall deputy rising from the dust, clutching the bandit's revolver, and the bandit, licked and holding his wrenched wrist, sitting abjectly at Lofty's feet.

Two of the passengers had rushed over to Annie and the unconscious girl. "She's all right—just fainted," Annie flung at them, and started after the fugitive ambusher.

A few seconds later she crashed through the brush and went out of sight, rifle in hand.

Old Tim Kelly was having his wounded arm bandaged by the third passenger, and watching Lofty snap a pair of handcuffs on the unmasked prisoner. He peered into the heavy-set ambusher's face and screwed up his own countenance in an expression of disgust. "No wonder this hombre wore a mask," he said to Lofty. "He sure looked better in it!"

Lofty nodded with a grin. "He'll look worse after he serves awhile in the Tumbleweed Wagon!"

He grabbed the prisoner's arm and led him toward the stage. "We'll just tie you up on top, mister, where you can get a good look at the scenery. It'll be the last you see of it for a while."

Over at the side of the road, the lady passenger was

recovering from her faint. One of the gentlemen was tenderly fanning her with his hat, while the other tried to get her to sip water from the water bag that he had brought from the stage.

She opened wide, violet-blue eyes at them and tried to sit up straight and compose herself properly. "I—I'm sorry I fainted," she murmured. "I didn't mean to, really."

"It's perfectly natural for a lady," one of them assured her gallantly. And the other agreed with a vigorous nod.

Lofty came up, removing his hat. "Did he get much from you, miss?"

Her eyes filled with tears as she looked up at him. "Every penny I had in the world." And then she covered her face with her slim white hands and sobbed gently. much to his dismay.

Annie could hear the man ahead of her crashing and floundering through the thick tangle of spiny cactus and sagebrush. He was evidently lost, judging from the way he wandered this way and that, apparently trying to find the horses he and his partner had staked out. "Must be a real greenhorn, or he'd have marked his trail," she thought.

Once or twice, she glimpsed his head above the tangled brush. Then suddenly his crashing and stamping stopped.

She stood on tiptoe and looked over the top of the nearest rock. Sure enough, he had gotten through the thicket and was now running across an open stretch toward a big clump of tall boulders. He disappeared around them.

She knew she would have to hurry now. Undoubtedly the horses were tied behind those rocks. But he would hear her coming through the last few yards of the thicket! She stopped.

He might have a rifle in his saddle scabbard and be waiting for her, if she tried to follow now. As a matter of fact, he might have heard her coming after him, and just be waiting now, rifle ready, to stop her the moment she came out of the thicket!

It looked as if she had lost him. Any moment she expected to hear him riding off fast from behind those boulders.

Then she heard him call out angrily, "Stand still, you jughead! Whoa, boy!" and the noise that came with the words sounded like a struggle between a horse that didn't want to be ridden and a man who was in a hurry to ride.

She grinned and pushed forward through the last few yards of thicket, rifle ready. He and the horse were making so much noise in their struggle that they couldn't have heard half a dozen lawmen galloping toward them all at once. She was grateful for the distraction.

By the time she had reached the clearing and was running toward the clump of boulders, the struggle was all over. The tall ambusher was in his saddle, behind the boulders, and had started riding over to where his partner's horse was peacefully grazing.

He leaned over to pick up its reins, but before his hand could close on them, he heard the click of Annie's rifle, and swung around in the saddle to see her standing only a few feet away with the weapon leveled at him.

She called out sharply, "Up with your hands! No tricks!"

"What, you again?" he said mockingly. She suspected that, behind his kerchief mask, he was more amused than alarmed. But he lazily put up his hands. "All right, miss," he said. "I'm doing it! Now what would you like me to do next?"

"You can get down off that horse, and keep your hands straight up!" she commanded, moving closer and holding her aim.

"Yes, miss." He sounded resigned, and still a little amused, but as he took his right foot out of the stirrup and started to swing out of the saddle, he rolled his spur lightly along the horse's flank.

The startled animal gave an indignant snort and reared on its hind legs, forefeet beating the air.

Annie took a quick step backward to get out of its way, and one of her spurs caught in an exposed root and tripped her. She tried to recover her balance but, to her angry surprise, she went sprawling on her back and lost her grip on the rifle. It fell into the sand beside her.

By the time she had scrambled to her feet again and grabbed up the rifle, the masked man had calmed down his horse, wheeled it, and was riding away up the trail. She saw him look back and wave his hat just before he went out of sight around a giant boulder.

"Go ahead an' laugh, Mr. Smart Aleck!" she said angrily, under her breath. "You're not in the clear yet!" She ran over to the other horse.

Before the hoofbeats of the masked man's mount had died in the distance, she was in the saddle and galloping after him at top speed, her rifle pocketed in the saddle holster.

She came in sight of him just as he rode up to the trail that wound along the side of Bobcat Hill. She knew that trail well. It had a lot of ups and downs before it finally led off down into the old wagon road across the desert toward the distant and sinister Black Buttes.

She decided that by riding through the valley below him, she could make better time than he could up on the trail. If their horses were pretty well matched for speed, she ought to be at the end of the trail ahead of him, and ready to stop him.

She slapped the stranger's horse with her hat and urged him on. "Get moving, horse! Let's see if you can run!"

The tall bandit looked back and down at Annie and waved. He was making a game of the race. He pounded along at a fast gallop, and Annie tried to hurry her horse to keep up with him. She soon realized that her mount was tiring, and the masked man was drawing ahead steadily.

"Come on, horse!" she begged, and slapped the reins against his neck. He gave an indignant snort, and for the next hundred yards he gave all he had to the gallop. Now she and the man on the upper trail were riding almost even.

Then she felt the horse under her begin to slow down, and she knew that she couldn't force him any more. He was a good little horse, and she didn't want to hurt him.

She drew the Winchester from the saddle boot, and without slackening her hold on the reins, she lifted the rifle to her shoulder and sighted along it at the horse and rider on the upper trail.

She was moving fast and so was the target, but it was her only chance to stop the bandit. Her finger pressed on the trigger, and the rifle crashed loudly.

Her aim was true. The bullet tore through the bandit's right-hand rein, and cut it in half. The front end whipped forward across the horse's face, and the terrified animal bolted. The man on his back lost control and was flung out of the saddle in a wide arc that landed him below the trail on the hillside.

Annie thought for a moment that she had missed the reins and hit the man, but then she saw the broken strap flapping as the horse took off fast and she breathed easier.

She dismounted hastily and ran up the slope to where the masked man was lying huddled between rocks. She carried her rifle, and kept it pointed in his direction as she moved close. He lay limp with his eyes closed.

She laid her rifle aside, close enough to grab it if he turned out to be faking. Then she knelt and lifted the kerchief from his face.

There was something vaguely familiar about it, but she couldn't place him. He looked like a man of thirty or so, and was clean-shaven. She thought, "Guess the reason he looks familiar, is that I've probably seen his face on Wanted posters."

He began to groan and move his head around. Annie suspected he would be conscious in a few minutes. She remembered seeing a rawhide lariat looped on the saddle of the horse she had been riding. It would take her only a minute or two to get it, and she would feel a lot easier with him tied up.

She tucked her rifle under her arm and made her way back down the hillside as rapidly as she could. Her horse was skittish, and every time she got close to him, he flicked his ears and rolled his eyes and cantered away. After a couple of minutes of this, she managed to coax him close with a handful of sweet grass. While he was nibbling on it, she got the lariat off his saddle and started back up the hill with it.

When she got to the spot where she had left the ambusher, he was gone.

She read the answer expertly from his tracks. He had sat up—there were the marks where he had rested on his elbows—then he had gotten to his feet, somewhat heavily from the deep marks his boot toes had made. And then he had followed her, staggering down the hill!

She started down cautiously, rifle ready, but at the foot of the hill the level ground was mostly flat rock, and she lost the footprints on it.

He could have gone in any direction, but Annie knew which way *she* would have headed in his situation. She would have gone straight for the horse!

She could see the animal still grazing. The bandit hadn't reached it yet. She moved forward, lifting her rifle ready to cover him at first sight.

Then a crashing sound in the heavy brush over at one side made her wheel in a flash, her rifle leveled. "Come out with your hands up, mister!" she called.

But no tall bandit stood up. Instead, she saw a rock rolling and bouncing down out of that clump of brush, leaving a tiny cloud of dust to show where it had landed a few seconds before.

She realized at once that he had thrown that rock to make her look for him in that direction. He had used practically the same trick she had used on him and his partner, back at the stage holdup! And she had been taken in by it, just as he had!

She wheeled quickly again, and was just in time to see

the horse being pulled by his reins over back of a tall
boulder. A moment later, the tall bandit rode out into the
open, slapping the horse into action with his hat.

She lowered her rifle and stared after him helplessly. She
couldn't chase him. She had no horse. He had outmaneu-
vered her. Not only had she failed to capture him, but here
she was, miles from anywhere, in high-heeled riding boots.
She'd have a long walk!

Then she had an inspiration. The horse whose reins she
had shot apart might be grazing somewhere near. It was
tired, and she didn't think it would have run very far after
dumping its rider. If she could locate it, maybe the stagecoach loot would be in its saddlebags. And so might that
envelope of Uncle Luke's that they had taken from Lofty!

4   A Lady in Distress

Annie hurriedly set her rifle down and started to climb to the top of the highest boulder. It was hard to find a toe hold on its slick granite sides, but after slipping and sliding a bit, and getting out of breath, she managed to reach the flat top and pull herself up over the edge so she could look for the runaway horse.

Then she discovered that she had had all that exercise for nothing. The tall outlaw was just disappearing into the distance along the narrow wagon road winding toward the faraway buttes. He was leading the second horse behind him.

"He certainly doesn't miss any bets!" she thought crossly. "Now I have to climb right down again, and probably scuff my boots worse this time!"

She got down a lot faster than she had climbed up, and

when she reached the ground she heard a shout of, "Hey, Annie! We're here!"

Tagg and Lofty were riding fast toward her. Lofty had cut loose one of the stage horses and was riding it bareback, while Tagg tried valiantly to keep up with him on Pixie, and led Annie's Target.

She couldn't help thinking, "Too bad they didn't make it a few minutes sooner!" But she was glad to see them anyhow. It would save her a long hike in riding boots.

Lofty galloped up as she came forward to meet them. "Where's the ambusher? Where's he tied up?"

She shook her head. "No place! He's gone!"

Lofty stared at her as if he couldn't quite believe it. "You mean he got away from you?"

"Clean away! He outslickered me!"

"Golly!" Tagg sounded both amazed and shocked.

Annie saw how he felt. She put her arm over his shoulders and smiled down into his face. "We can't win all the battles, punkin!"

"We heard a shot. Did you—*miss?*" He could hardly get that dreadful word out. Annie missing a shot was about the same to Tagg as the sun forgetting to rise.

"Well, no," she smiled. "I hit what I aimed for, sure

enough. But it didn't stop him." She could see Tagg let out a sigh of relief. "He's a smart one!"

"Anyhow, I got his pardner!" Lofty boasted. "And tomorrow Luke and I will go after this one. Too bad you lost him, but don't worry, we'll bring him back before he gets too far off!"

Annie kept back a giggle. She had had to help Lofty out of several tight spots in the past when he had tangled with lawbreakers, but apparently it hadn't hurt his opinion of himself compared to a mere female! "Of course you will," she agreed meekly, but with a twinkle in her eyes.

"Did the young lady get over her scare?"

"Reckon so," Lofty nodded. "When we started after you, she was looking better."

"That's good! I was a little worried when she keeled over the way she did on top of my rifle. I reckon she's the timid kind that faints at the drop of a hat."

"Well, it's only natural for a lady to be afraid of guns," Lofty defended the newcomer.

Annie looked startled. That sounded like a slap at *her*. Then she noticed Lofty's dreamy expression and realized he didn't mean it the way it sounded.

She hoped Tagg wouldn't fly to her defense, but when

she turned to look at him, he had the same dreamy expression on his freckled face, and was saying, "She sure is a pretty lady, isn't she? Her name's Miss Murdock, an' she comes from Boston, an' she's going to live in Diablo with her brother. And she has dark blue eyes."

"They're more violet color," Lofty disagreed, "and they sure go nice with her brown hair."

"Well, you boys don't miss much, do you?" Annie teased.

"Uh—I—uh—" Lofty looked a little sheepish. Then he caught the twinkle in Annie's eyes, and he grinned and winked at her. "It's a lawman's job to get all the facts, Sheriff Luke tells me!"

"You win!" Annie laughed. But she thought to herself, "That Lofty! Every new girl in town's the most beautiful, till another one arrives!"

Tagg asked suddenly, "Did the ambushers steal much gold from the stage?"

"There wasn't any aboard," Lofty replied, "or we'd have had a shotgun guard on the box."

"Then why did they hold it up? Was it that envelope they were after?" Annie asked.

"Sure looks that way," he answered glumly. "Wonder

how they knew I was bringing it from Bonanza City. Somebody on the Wanted list must have found out somehow."

"Maybe Uncle Luke can get it out of the prisoner you
caught," Annie suggested, and Lofty agreed he certainly
hoped so.

But beyond admitting that his name was Deuce Adams,
the prisoner would tell the sheriff nothing. To all the lawman's questions he had only a snicker and an insolent stare
for answer.

"All right. Have it your way," the sheriff finally told
him. "When we bring in your partner tomorrow, he may
be willing to tell us where you found out about that envelope
my deputy was bringing to me."

"You won't catch Bill. He's too smart for you," Deuce
sneered.

"Maybe." The sheriff leaned back in his chair and hooked
his thumbs in his suspenders. "Anyway, we've got you all
neatly bundled up for the Tumbleweed Wagon. I hear
they'll be rollin' in pronto."

Deuce Adams stiffened. "Yeah? Who says so?"

"Ask the same man who told you about that envelope!"
Sheriff Luke turned to Lofty. "Tuck him away, Lofty!"

As Lofty marched the prisoner back to the cells, Sheriff

Luke frowned at his thoughts. He knew that Deuce Adams had been picked up by the Tumbleweed Wagon some time in his career. The look in Deuce's eyes had told him that. If the wagon did show up in a few days, as he hoped it would, Deuce might be willing to talk to get out of riding in it.

The roving prison wagon was a bugaboo to the tumbleweed badmen that it gathered up. They had to work hard for their food, while the wagon wandered across the Territory. When they were finally unloaded at Bonanza City or some other town that had a big jail, they had labored at everything including road-clearing, ditch-digging, and wood-chopping. And after all that, they had to stand trial for their crimes. The loss of the envelope was a serious one to the sheriff of Diablo. He had waited nearly three months for its contents to arrive from Texas. There should have been enough information in it to jail at least a dozen of the tough characters who had shown up lately in Diablo and who seemed to intend to make it their permanent headquarters.

If there was any possible chance of finding the fugitive ambusher and getting the envelope back from him, it would be worth a vigorous search.

But a little later, when he questioned Annie about the man's escape, he was pretty doubtful.

She pointed to the big hand-drawn map on the office wall. "He was headed up toward the buttes, last time I saw him. With two horses, riding first one and then the other, he must be almost there by now."

Her uncle nodded gloomily. "I suppose we'd be wasting time trying to trail him through that rocky country. I doubt if I could even raise a posse who'd be willing to try!"

"I'll go with you, if you'd like me-to, Uncle Luke!" Annie suggested eagerly. "I could study the hoofprints where their two horses were waiting during the holdup, and maybe find some mark like a broken shoe-nail that I could watch for along the trail!"

"Never mind, honey," the sheriff seemed discouraged. "Anyhow, like as not we'd be riding into a hornets' nest up in the buttes."

"What I can't figure is who spread the word that we were getting those Wanted handbills up from Texas!" Lofty groaned.

"I can't figure it. It's been over a month—closer to six weeks, in fact—since the council had me write to Austin for them, but I'm right sure nobody on the council has told what we were up to. They're all as anxious as we are to run the riffraff out of town."

"Maybe one of them let it slip by accident," Annie suggested.

The sheriff considered it and then shook his head. "It wasn't Sam Gillis, I'm sure of that. He's the one suggested having the handbills sent to the United States marshal's office in Bonanza City, so they wouldn't be spotted in the Diablo mail. I know he'd hold his tongue."

"Unless Mrs. Gillis wormed it out of him somehow," Annie wrinkled her nose and grinned at them.

Her uncle shook his head. "He knows better than to talk to her about anything he doesn't want spread out wide!"

"Chet Alberts is pretty close-mouthed, too," Lofty checked the council off on his fingers, "and Doc Busby, and Mayor Drury."

"Well, we'll have the answer when the Tumbleweed Wagon rolls in and Deuce gets a good long look at it!" Sheriff Luke said with conviction.

"If he doesn't weaken, I guess we'll just have to send away for a new batch of Wanted handbills, and put off our gun-hawk roundup till they get here!" Lofty prophesied.

"And by then, the town'll really be overrun. And the Tumbleweed Wagon long gone to other parts of the Territory!"

The Diablo Hotel lobby was small and dingy. The fumes of liquor and tobacco smoke drifted in from the partly open door of the barroom that took up one corner of the hotel.

The young lady of the stage holdup sat up straight and prim on the hard bench near the front door, and tried to act as if she didn't hear the rough laughter and raucous voices that burst out of the barroom every now and then.

Each time the front door opened, she turned hopeful eyes toward it, only to sink back disappointed.

Sam Gillis was watching her from his post behind the hotel desk. His wife Essie owned the hotel and made him work as clerk and combination bellboy and chambermaid. He hated the job, the hotel, and sometimes Essie, who was a large woman with a bad temper and a loud voice. She was also the town gossip.

Sam had felt sorry for the young woman when her brother, whom she had expected to meet at the stage station, failed to show up. He had offered her the temporary shelter of the hotel's lobby. He was rather curious to see

the brother. He couldn't remember anyone whose name was Blair Murdock, in and around Diablo. Still, all sorts came and went every day.

He only hoped her brother would show up soon. There were no rooms for young women in the hotel. In fact, there were no rooms left for anyone. By midnight even the lobby would be crowded with sleepers, sprawled across chairs and rolled up on the floor in their blankets. It had happened almost every night since the Soapstone diggings had opened.

The young lady was quite evidently not the kind that should be sitting around a hotel lobby alone. He decided he had better do something about it before the place started getting noisy.

The night clerk was having his supper in the kitchen, before going on duty. Sam called him in to watch the desk. "Look out for things till I get back," he told the young man.

The clerk cocked a thumb toward the young woman, "What about her?" he asked in a low voice.

Sam Gillis shrugged. "Dunno. I'm goin' over and lay it in Luke MacTavish's lap. Maybe he knows where to find the brother she's waitin' for."

But at the sheriff's office, no one, including Annie and Tagg, had heard of anyone named Murdock.

"Did she send him word when she'd get here?" Annie asked.

"She says she wired him two weeks ago, when she changed stages at Granite Creek."

"What address did she send the telegram to?" Luke queried. "The hotel?"

"No, the telegraph office, she says."

Annie cocked her head to one side. "Maybe he didn't get the message! If he didn't—she'll be sitting there the rest of the night!"

"Oh, no, she won't! Somebody's got to git her out of there before the boys start cuttin' up! Things get a mite rough sometimes, an' I don't want her around there."

Annie grabbed her hat and started to the door. "I'll be right back. I'm going to talk to Hebediah Jenks at the telegraph office." She was gone in a flash.

She waited impatiently as the old telegraph operator slowly thumbed through the yellow "flimsies," copies of the past month's telegrams. "Don't find it here in the 'Delivereds,'" he said. "I'll look in the 'Not Delivereds.'"

Mr. Jenks moved to the next steel hook hanging over

his desk. There were only a few slips on that one. He pulled them off one by one, with a careful look at each.

Impatiently Annie looked over his shoulder. Suddenly she reached over and put her finger on the next one as he took it off the hook. "There! It's addressed to Blair Murdock, Diablo!"

"Hold on there, Miss Annie!" He brushed her hand away, and held the paper so she couldn't read it. "Public ain't permitted to handle the records. Shoo!" And he settled his specs more firmly on his nose and slowly read the telegram through to himself.

When he had finished, he peered at her over the tops of his glasses. "What did you say the sender's name is?"

"Melinda Murdock," she said firmly. "Isn't that it?"

"It could be," he admitted grudgingly, squinting at it from first one angle and then another. "Melinda somethin'. Can't quite make out my own squiggles."

"I'd better show it to her." Annie held out her hand.

"No, siree!" He held it away from her. "Comp'ny property. Stays here till addressee calls for it. Regulation number five-six-two. But you can tell her it hasn't been picked up yet."

"All right," Annie started slowly toward the door. "And

thanks, Mr. Jenks." She stopped and looked back. "If a man comes and asks for his telegram and says he's Blair Murdock, please tell him his sister is waiting for him at the hotel."

"He'd better hurry," Mr. Jenks said flatly, "because I'm puttin' up the shutters in seven and a half minutes, no more an' no less!"

"What now?" Annie wondered, as she looked up and down the little main street. Then she made up her mind.

Instead of going back to her uncle's office, she went straight to the Gillis Hotel. Loud bursts of noise and men's coarse voices came out of the barroom on the hotel corner, and she had to step off the wooden sidewalk twice to make way for groups of jovial miners who were out to celebrate and spend their hard-earned gold dust.

In the hotel lobby, Sam Gillis and his clerk were behind the desk. Gillis caught her eye as she came in, and he looked questioningly toward Miss Murdock. Annie answered by a quick shake of her head as she went over to the young woman.

"Hi, there!" she greeted her. "I was wondering how you were getting along."

"I—I'll be all right when my brother arrives to pick me up." Melinda Murdock tried to sound calm and self-assured, but there was panic behind her polite tones.

Annie didn't want to worry her, but she had to tell her the truth. "Your telegram is still waiting for your brother at the telegraph office, Miss Murdock."

"Oh!" The young woman turned pale and Annie was afraid she was going to faint again. She sat down quickly beside her, but Miss Murdock pulled herself together after a moment, and even tried to smile. "Then he won't be coming for me tonight!" She started the words lightly, but her voice broke, and when she turned to Annie, there were big tears in her eyes. "But he told me he'd be waiting for my wire. He said he'd have a place at his mining claim all fixed up for us."

"If he's a miner, that sort of accounts for it. They get so busy digging, they don't pay any attention to what day it is or anything. He'll probably remember it all of a sudden and come sky-hootin' in one day, soon, looking for you!"

But Melinda shook her head. "He told me to get here the first week in May, because the weather would be good. So he was expecting me." She burst into heavy sobs. "Something must have happened to him! Something terrible!"

5   One Problem Taken Care Of

"If anything has happened to your brother, Miss Murdock," Annie told her quietly, "my uncle the sheriff will know about it. Maybe I'd better go talk to him."

Melinda Murdock stood up quickly as another burst of raucous laughter and the sounds of a scuffle came from the corner barroom. She brushed the tears from her eyes and drew her cape around her shoulders. "I'll go with you, if you don't mind, Miss Oakley."

"That'd be better," Annie agreed, with a disgusted look toward the partly open barroom door.

Sam Gillis and his night clerk, Jake, exchanged looks of relief as the two girls headed for the door. Sam hurried around the front of the desk to open the door for them. "I'm sorry I had no room here for you, miss," he told Melinda politely, "but I guess the sheriff'll find a place for you to wait that's more suitable than this."

"I should hope so!" Annie commented, and hurried Melinda outside.

Sam Gillis' friendly smile faded as he looked after them. The less he saw of Annie Oakley and her relatives and friends, the better he liked it. He was tired of making believe he was on the sheriff's side. Well, pretty soon he'd show his real colors, and there'd be a new deal all around!

He turned away with a scowl and went back to the desk. "If there's anything I don't like, it's having women settin' around where trouble's li'ble to break out any minute!" he told the night clerk. "I'm glad the Oakley girl had enough sense to git her out of here."

Jake chewed the end of a pen. "Feel kinda sorry for her, at that. Like as not the poor thing has come to the wrong town, or even the wrong Territory! Women never get anything right! That feller she's waitin' for is liable right now to be in Mexico or Alaska!" He laughed with Gillis and they both felt a few sizes bigger.

Sam Gillis started across the lobby, but Jake called out plaintively, "Say, Mr. Gillis, do you still aim to go fishin' tomorrow?"

"Sure!" Gillis scowled at his clerk. "Why shouldn't I?

It's good fishin' weather, and I guess I got a right to take a day off when I want to!"

Jake explained hurriedly, "I was only thinkin' about those outlaws that held up the stage. One of 'em is still runnin' loose, an' you might come across him!"

"Huh!" Jake grinned. "Not much chance of it! He's a long way off by now. And anyhow, he wouldn't be fool enough to figger a lone fisherman would be carryin' anything worth stealin'!"

"I dunno." Jake was still not convinced it was safe.

"Well, *I* do!" Sam answered, with a swagger. He sauntered on into the barroom, leaving the clerk gloomily looking forward to double duty for the next twenty-four hours. Sam Gillis would be sorry he hadn't stayed in town and given up the fishing, if he ran into that outlaw. And Jake rather hoped he would! He wouldn't talk so big any more.

Down the street at the sheriff's office, Melinda Murdock was reading her brother's last letter to a sympathetic audience that included Lofty as well as Annie, Tagg, and Sheriff MacTavish.

Her brother had written it at Bonanza City, on the eve of a trip to Diablo to register a mining claim that he had staked out in the hills above Diablo a short time before.

He planned to be in Diablo the first week in May, and told
her to meet him there then. He had high hopes that his
claim would pay off richly. There was an assessor in
Bonanza City to whom he had shown the ore samples he
had dug out, and the man had said that they were some
of the richest he had ever tested. The letter ended with
instructions to send him a telegram in Diablo when she
was sure which day she would arrive on the stage.

"So I did, two weeks ago! And he still hasn't picked it
up!" she said unhappily.

"There's nothing to worry about, child," the kindly
sheriff told her. "He probably had to change his plans about
when he'd get here. Maybe something came up at the claim
and he couldn't leave. But I'm sure he'll show up soon."

"I just know something has happened to him!" she
insisted.

"If it had, we'd have had a report about it here," Lofty
assured her, pointing to the sheriff's record book open on
the desk, "and you can see for yourself, there's no mention."

"Maybe he has nobody to take care of the claim while
he's away," Annie suggested, to comfort her.

"That could be," Sheriff Luke agreed. Then he told
Melinda, "My advice would be to just stop worrying, and

settle down to wait till he shows up. Maybe it'll only be a few days or a couple of weeks at the most."

"But—" Melinda hesitated, then continued sadly, "I can't wait around—even a few days. I haven't a cent to my name. Those holdup men today took my last dollar. Unless I can find some kind of job right away, I don't know what I am going to do."

"Don't you worry about getting a job, Miss Murdock. You're coming straight out to the ranch with us and stay as long as you want to while you're waiting for your brother!" Annie told her eagerly.

"We've got lots of room!" Tagg added. And the sheriff nodded quick agreement, with a warm smile.

But the young woman sat up straight and shook her head slowly. "Thanks, everyone, but I couldn't impose on you. I'll find a position here in town, doing something, and just wait till Blair gets here."

Annie and her uncle exchanged worried looks, and then Annie said matter-of-factly, "Just about what did you have in mind, Miss Murdock? There isn't much a young lady can do around here."

"Why, I don't really know," Melinda said faintly. "I can cook a little—and keep house—and—" but she couldn't seem to think of anything more. She made a helpless little gesture and looked appealingly at them. "I—I guess I don't know how to do anything they pay people wages for."

"Waiting on table—cooking in a short-order lunchroom," Lofty counted it off with a serious face, "washing and ironing for the miners. No, that's taken care of by the Chinese laundry." He shook his head. "None of those seem to fit."

"I should say not!" Annie glared indignantly at him.

"How about playing the organ at our church? I could do the pumpin'! Pastor says I'm a whiz of a pumper!" Tagg boasted.

"Two dollars a Sunday, and a dollar each for weddings and funerals," Annie's eyes twinkled, "that wouldn't pay many bills, button."

"I wouldn't be worth even that much," Melinda smiled faintly at them. "I can't play a note."

"I got it!" Lofty interrupted with a wide grin. "Diablo needs a schoolteacher! How about that, Luke?"

Luke nodded gravely. "We don't have one," he admitted, "and we could use one."

Annie clapped her hands. "That's a wonderful idea!"

Everyone, even Melinda, was smiling. But Tagg's smile started to fade quickly, as he realized what it meant. He looked glumly from one to the other and his face knitted up into a scowl. He kicked the floor with his heel, and when Annie looked at him to see why, he scowled at her. "We don't need any ol' teacher," he said defiantly, "because it's vacation."

Annie shook a stern finger at him. "There's still a month and a half to go before real vacation starts! So we *do* need a teacher!" She turned to Melinda Murdock, "Uncle Luke is on the school board, Miss Murdock. I'm sure he can arrange it for you, if you want him to."

Melinda turned to the sheriff, her blue-violet eyes wide with hope. "Oh, would you, Sheriff? I'd be so grateful! And then, it wouldn't matter if Blair couldn't get here for weeks!"

"Well, I'm only one vote on the board," he smiled at them both, "but I'll do my best. I think you can count on the job."

He rose and reached for his broad-brimmed hat. "I'll get over to Chick Bergen's livery stable and borrow that old buggy of his, so we can take your trunk and bags out to the ranch."

"Thank you, Sheriff, but I won't need the trunk. It can wait here in the stage depot till Blair comes to take me out to our own place."

"Anything you say, my dear," the sheriff gave her a reassuring smile. But he was thinking, *"If* he's able to get here. There are a lot of things that could have happened to him, alone on a rich claim."

Sam Gillis stood behind the batwing doors of the barroom in his hotel, and looked out into the street. He saw the tall sheriff ride out first in the direction of the ranch, and then a little later, he saw the livery stable rig go by with Annie handling the reins, and the Murdock girl seated beside her, looking around at everything with a lot of interest. The boy Tagg, who was never far from his sister, brought up the rear, riding his pony and leading Annie's fine little horse Target.

Someone else had come up beside Gillis and was looking at them, too, over Sam's shoulder. Tex Chantry was a tall, thin-faced man with the cold hard eyes of the professional gambler. He wore well-tailored dark clothes of good material, and sported a flashing diamond ring that matched the stickpin in his black tie.

"That's quite a parade," he said dryly.

Sam Gillis nodded and spoke without turning his head. "Shall I mosey over to the jail and try to get a word with Deuce?"

The gambler scowled. "No! Keep away from him for a few days, and let him think over how stupid he was to let himself get arrested!"

"But I hear that the Tumbleweed Wagon's due next week!" Gillis was worried. "We oughta set him loose before it gets here."

"I hadn't heard it was headed this way," Chantry said, frowning. The news seemed to worry him a little. Then he brushed it aside with a gesture of his hand. "We'll know when it gets close. Let him stay there till we do."

Gillis shrugged. "Okay, Tex. You're giving the orders."

"Get off early in the morning," Chantry ordered, "and when you get back with the envelope, bring it right to me." He moved away and sat down at a table against the wall. Bringing a pack of cards out of his pocket, he started to shuffle them. Tex Chantry could do marvelous things with those long white hands of his and a pack of cards. In the last few years they had made a good living for him in many a town between Texas and Idaho. But here in Diablo, with so many prospectors and miners drifting through with gold-dust-filled pockets, he had done best. He intended to stay awhile, and grow with the town!

When Sam Gillis had told him about the Wanted hand-bills the sheriff had sent for to Austin, his old stamping ground, he had decided to intercept the envelope before it got to the sheriff. He had no doubt that his own crooked past would catch up to him if he didn't. He remembered one handbill in particular that called him a card cheat, confidence man, and highway robber. If that one was in the sheriff's mail, he would have to leave town in short order.

So he hired Deuce Adams to ambush the stagecoach and get him the envelope before it could reach Diablo and Sheriff MacTavish.

All the way to the ranch, Melinda Murdock and Annie chattered and got acquainted, while Tagg rode Pixie and led Target behind the buggy.

When they reached the ranch, Annie tied the reins to the hitching post, and called to Tagg to put the buggy in the barn as soon as he had taken care of the horses. Then she took Melinda inside.

Melinda's eyes grew big and sparkling at sight of the comfortable, roomy living room with its colorful Navaho rugs and its fine old furniture that had come from the East with the sheriff's parents when he and Annie's mother were children.

"Your home is beautiful! It's so warm and—friendly!" she told Annie impulsively. "Oh, thank you so much for asking me to visit you."

"We're happy to have you," Annie assured her.

Sheriff Luke had started a crackling fire in the stone fireplace, and it was sending a welcome warmth toward the two girls, who had felt the early chill of desert darkness.

Melinda looked around her with a smile. "This is just the kind of home I hope Blair and I will have soon!"

Tagg found them all sitting around chatting when he came in from the barn. They looked a lot happier than he was feeling, but he perked up when he heard Annie say, "It'll be a lot of fun having you here, Melinda. Tagg and I'll take you horseback riding after school, and show you the country."

"I'm afraid I only know how to ride sidesaddle," Melinda told her, "and not very well at that!"

Tagg couldn't stay quiet. "What's sidesaddle?"

Uncle Luke smiled. "That's what Mrs. Sam Gillis was talking about last week when she told Annie here that she should ride like a lady and not astraddle like a man!"

Annie laughed with him, and then explained to Melinda, "Mrs. Gillis is chairman of the school board, and she thinks she has to run a lot of things besides the school. But she means well, I'm sure."

"I—I hope she'll think I'm qualified to teach the school," Melinda's pretty forehead puckered up.

"I don't know why she'd think anything else!" Annie assured her.

But at the school board meeting the next day, it wasn't easy to convince Mrs. Gillis that the very pretty applicant would make a good teacher for the young of Diablo. The other members of the board were enthusiastic after hearing where Melinda had attended school in the East, and very much impressed by her engraved diploma from the Finishing School for Ladies.

"Education ain't everything," Mrs. Gillis said primly. "I got to be sure she's fit to teach the young'uns how to behave. She don't look strong enough to wallop 'em."

"Maybe they won't need wallopin' if they get the right

bringin' up at home," Mrs. Chet Alberts suggested meaningly. The Gillises had two teen-age boys who had done more than their share of cutting up to plague the last teacher.

Mrs. Gillis glared, but Sarah Alberts stared back at her and refused to be intimidated.

"Ladies, shall we vote on Miss Murdock?" Sheriff Luke asked patiently.

"I vote Yes!" Mrs. Alberts announced, and was echoed by everyone but Mrs. Gillis, who closed her jaw and wouldn't speak.

"Oh, come on, Essie!" It was the mayor's good-natured wife. "You'd rather have her than let the kids run wild for five or six months while we wait for someone else to show up that might suit you better!"

"All right!" Mrs. Gillis threw up her hands. "But she's got to be warned that there'll be no flibbertigibbeting around, going to dances, making sheep's eyes at the men like Miss Smith did. First time she does anything to get herself talked about disrespectful, out she goes!"

"She'll toe the mark, ladies," Sheriff Luke assured them. "You won't be sorry you hired her."

"Hmph!" Mrs. Gillis' lips were set in a straight line.

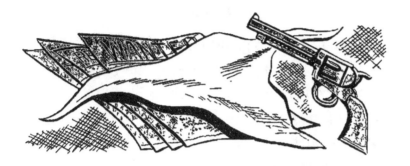

6   The Halfway House

It was still dark outside the frame house on the outskirts of Diablo, when Sam Gillis stole out of his attic room and tiptoed downstairs and past his wife's bedroom on the second floor. He was carrying his boots and his fishing rod and tackle.

He paused a moment outside her door to listen, but her hearty snores convinced him that she hadn't heard him stirring around. It would have been too bad for his plans if he had awakened her. Essie Gillis would have refused to allow him to go, when there were so many things to attend to at the hotel and around their home.

He hurried to Chick Bergen's livery stable, where his horse boarded, and aroused that gentleman by rapping on the stable door. Chick let him in, with much sleepy grumbling about people who were crazy enough to get up in the middle of the night to go fishing.

Sam Gillis took it good-naturedly, and even apologized to the livery stable man for disturbing him. "I'll bring you a mess of good eatin' to make up for it," he promised.

But he thought, instead, "When Tex Chantry gets things runnin' his way here in town, Chick'll be glad to jump when I say the word!" The thought of his own importance in that approaching day was a comforting thing to dwell on, as he started out on the long, hot journey across the desert valley toward the distant Black Buttes.

It wasn't that Chantry had made him any definite promise about being mayor, but he had hinted it a couple of times lately.

It amused Sam to think how surprised Essie would be when things started popping around Diablo, and he got to be a big man, instead of an unpaid servant in her hotel.

He could almost forget the dry, choking dust of the desert as his horse plodded along.

After several hours, he came to the foot of the buttes. There was a green spot where a small spring bubbled, and Sam Gillis dismounted to rest.

There was a clump of boulders a hundred yards away, and behind them the start of a steep trail that would tax his tired horse's strength unless it had a chance to rest awhile.

It was only the second time that Gillis had made the journey to the notorious outlaw hide-out that the men who stopped there from time to time had nicknamed Halfway House. It wasn't halfway to anywhere. It was more like halfway to nowhere, because most of the lodgers who drifted in and out were men who had been "someplace" and were hurriedly heading toward "no place" with the law hot on their heels.

Tex Chantry had brought him up here with him to meet Deuce Adams, who spent most of his time at the house as a sort of caretaker. They hadn't met Deuce's "partner" at that time, because he had been on a hunting trip for the house's venison supply.

It would have been pleasant to linger here till the cool of the day; but Gillis knew he had better move on up to the house on his errand, or he would have to make the longest return part of the trip through pitch-black desert night in which he might easily lose his way.

The steep trail wound up into the buttes that towered straight up on each side of him. It took him along narrow ledges that made him stare up at the sky so he wouldn't get

dizzy and lose his nerve. The road surface was granite, and
every step of his horse's iron shoes echoed back as if half a
dozen riders were on all sides.

He wasn't surprised when, turning a corner of the trail,
he heard a faint, plaintive owl-hoot. He glanced up in the
direction it came from, and saw no owl.

He pulled to a stop without waiting, and answered the
call with a "Whoo-hoo!" just as soft and sad as the one
he was copying.

A moment later, he heard a rustle of brush just above
his head, and when he looked up, he saw a bearded face
thrust over the edge of a tall boulder beside the trail. The
nose of a six-shooter pointed down at him. "Whatcha want,
bud?"

"It's me, Sam Gillis," he said hastily, "Tex Chantry's
friend. He sent me to talk to Deuce's pardner."

"Bill Welton, you mean?" the face inquired.

"If Welton's the jasper that rode with Deuce yesterday,
he's the one I'm talkin' about."

"He's up there," the lookout cocked a thumb up-trail.
"Go ahead. And say, tell Cookie to bring down my dinner
pronto, or I'll be up and stomp on his neck!"

The raucous caw-caw of a crow echoed loudly around the

steep walls as Sam Gillis started up a narrow draw. He knew that his arrival was being signaled to whoever was up at Halfway House.

At the end of the draw, an abrupt right-angle turn brought him to the wide clearing in which a strongly built, old log cabin squatted.

Halfway House had small, narrow windows without glass. They were very little more than loopholes, for defense of the cabin when it was under siege. There had been several times in its forty-year existence when guns had blazed out of those windows against Indians. And the house had never fallen to attack.

White men, too, had tried to destroy the house during those long years. There were still a dozen or more slugs of lead imbedded in its thick, single-plank door, along with an assortment of arrowheads.

A big chimney arose on the north side, and as Gillis crossed the empty clearing, leading his horse, an appetizing smell came to him from the thin smoke he could see curling out of it.

There were four horses in the pole corral alongside the south end of the house. And four saddles hung on the rail.

He stopped a few yards from the house, wondering if

he should put his horse in the corral without an invitation. Then, as he turned that way, he saw the front door of the big cabin open and a tall, almost gaunt young man came out and strode toward him.

"I'm Gillis, friend of Tex Chantry's," he parroted, "lookin' for a feller called Bill Welton."

"I'm Welton," the tall young man said shortly. "Where have they got Deuce?" He wasted no time welcoming Gillis.

"He's in the calaboose!" Gillis was annoyed at the young man's cool manner. "It's where he belongs," he added spitefully, "for gettin' himself arrested by that fool deputy."

Bill Welton scowled down at him. "The deputy had some help we hadn't counted on, Gillis. Some girl sharpshooter moved in on us, and it was all I could do, myself, to get away from her!"

"That was the sheriff's niece, Annie Oakley."

"Well, whoever she is, she's too good a shot with her rifle! She smashed my gun to pieces, cut my reins with a bullet while we were both riding at a gallop, and if I hadn't had good luck, she'd have handed me over to her uncle trussed up like a Christmas turkey."

"You won't have to worry about her much longer!"

Gillis boasted. "Tex an' me have got some plans for Diablo when we take over. And one of them is a new sheriff, pronto!"

The tall young man smiled coldly, and Sam Gillis' round, weak face reddened. He could see that Welton was not impressed.

"I came for that envelope Tex hired you men to pick up," Sam said aggressively. Then, spitefully, "Or did Annie Oakley get it away from you?"

Bill Welton's expression didn't change. "It's yours if you've brought the two hundred dollars Chantry and Deuce agreed on as the price."

"*Two* hundred?" Gillis shook his head. "Seems to me it was a hundred."

Bill Welton's cold smile faded. His blue eyes were like marbles as he said softly, "Two hundred. You know it, so don't try to cut yourself in, or you'll never see the envelope. And I don't think Chantry would like that."

Gillis swallowed hard, and then he managed a weak laugh. "I was just kiddin'. Here's the dust." He drew a small deerskin pouch out of his coat pocket and showed it briefly to Bill Welton before he dropped it back. "You got the envelope?"

Bill Welton relaxed, and his smile was much warmer as he said, "Let's go in. Cookie's got grub on the table for a couple of pilgrims who are just passing through. We'll talk business after you eat."

The house had three rooms, one a large combination living room, kitchen, and bunkhouse for the passing guests. One was a storeroom for food, guns, and ammunition, most of it for sale at a good price to the men who came looking for help against the law. The third was a bunk room for the cook, Deuce Adams, and for the last couple of months, Bill Welton.

The cook was a peppery little man whose name had long ago been forgotten. That suited him very well, considering that it had been a little too well-known at one time. "Cookie" had been one of a gang of train robbers, and the only one of them who had escaped from the clutches of the law. He had drifted up to the house five years ago, found out that there was a spot for a good cook, and stayed on.

Cookie recognized Sam Gillis when he came in with Bill Welton, and made him welcome. But two other men who were seated at the long pine table, eating heartily of Cookie's stew, only threw suspicious glances at him and then went back to their silent meal.

Sam eyed them curiously as he and Bill Welton sat down at the table, but no one made a move to introduce them, so he decided not to ask any questions.

When the two had finished their meal, they each grabbed a couple of sour-dough biscuits from the baking pan and tucked them into their pockets. Then each dropped a silver dollar into the small Indian wicker basket on one end of the table, grunted some sort of brief thanks in Cookie's direction, nodded to the others, and went out.

A few minutes later, the three men heard them ride away.

Cookie dumped the two silver coins from the basket, balanced them in his hand, decided they were the right weight to be honest coins, and dropped them into his pocket. Then he slid the basket along the table so that it stopped in front of Sam Gillis.

"Help yourself to more grub, Gillis," Cookie told him, "and if you need any supplies, Bill can get them out of the storeroom for you. Give you a right good price on 'em, too."

"Thanks," Sam said sourly, "but I'm not needin' anything."

Cookie gave a last meaningful glance at the basket on the table, and retired to the bunk room to let them talk.

Sam's appetite having been satisfied, he pushed aside the

tin dishes and brought out the small leather bag of gold dust. He kept hold of it as he asked, "Now, where's that envelope?"

Bill Welton brought it out of his coat pocket and showed it to him. It was tightly sealed along the flap with blobs of dark red sealing wax, each showing the imprint of a Texas star, sign of the law.

Envelope and bag of gold dust changed hands.

Welton opened the bag and dumped the contents into a clean tin saucer. He stirred the shining dust with his finger, and was satisfied that it was the agreed-on amount without any worthless pebbles included to add to the weight. Then he poured it back into the little sack and pulled the strings tight.

Sam picked at one of the seals with his thumb. He would have liked to peek into the envelope before he gave it to Tex Chantry.

Bill Welton smiled. "Go ahead. Open it. I'd like to see, myself, what's in there. Might be a picture of me or Deuce."

Sam shook his head. "Nope," he said, "can't do it, Welton. Tex paid for it unopened. That's how he gets it."

Welton dangled the gold sack from his index finger, letting it swing in front of Sam suggestively. "I might be willing to pay a little, say twenty or so out of this dust, to look inside that envelope."

Sam was strongly tempted, but the thought of losing Chantry's friendship was even stronger. "Can't do it," he sighed, "can't do it."

A couple of hours later, when his horse had rested, Gillis was ready to ride back to Diablo.

Bill Welton walked to the corral with him and watched him mount. "How long are you boys down there planning to let Deuce stay in jail?" he asked quietly.

Gillis shrugged. "Tex says it'll do him good to sit it out awhile."

"How long is awhile?" There was a sharp edge to Welton's voice, but Gillis didn't notice it.

"Hard to say," he answered carelessly. "Tex gives the orders."

"Then tell him not to take too long about it. Deuce is a good friend of mine and I don't like the idea of letting him sit in jail!"

He scowled at Gillis, and the smaller man settled in his saddle and looked over the fence at him with a friendly smile. "Now don't get riled up, Welton," he said pleasantly.

"We'll have him out an' away before the Tumbleweed Wagon rolls in."

Welton looked startled. "The wagon? How close is it?"

Gillis waved carelessly. "Oh, several days out! We'll know in plenty of time to fix up a jailbreak the night before it's due!"

"See that you keep that in mind!" Welton said coldly.

"Sure!" Gillis grinned and started away. He saw Welton watching him unsmilingly when he turned to wave before he cantered down the trail. And as he rode, he thought angrily, "Who does he think he is, giving me an' Tex orders? Maybe we'll just let Deuce sit there an' wait for the wagon!"

7   Some Questions and Answers

Bill Welton walked back into the cabin. Cookie was cleaning up the rickety old stove, slamming pots and pans around and muttering angrily to himself. Gillis, it seemed, had ridden off without dropping anything in the basket.

"He's a runty tumblebug and a cheapskate!" he exploded to Bill Welton.

Welton thought for a moment. "Would you take his word if he promised something?"

"Not unless it was going to pay *him* off plenty!" Cookie slammed the stove-lid in place so hard it bounced off the stove, hit the floor, and rolled across the room.

Welton nodded slowly. That had been his estimate of Sam Gillis, too—a man who talked big but couldn't be trusted.

"Ouch!" Cookie had tried to pick up the hot stove-lid

and had burned his fingers. He kicked it the rest of the way across the dirt floor to the stove. "You can stay there, for all of me!" he snarled at it. Then he turned scowling to Welton, nursing his burned fingers, and barked, "You're all alike! I get no thanks for anything!"

"Here," Bill Welton handed him the pot of bacon grease from the back of the stove, "stick your fingers in that. It'll take the sting out!"

Cookie grunted, and obeyed, still scowling.

"Feel better?" Welton asked.

Cookie nodded, and a grin spread on his homely face as he looked, at the tall young man. "I didn't mean that for you, Bill. Just the rest."

"People don't think, that's all. It happens I know that I'd be dead if it hadn't been for you and Deuce taking care of me the last couple of months!"

"Yeah!" Cookie grinned, "I wouldn'ta give two cents for your chances, the day Deuce found you out in the desert and carted you all the way up here across his saddle. That bullet gash in your scalp was a bad one!"

Bill Welton touched a red, painful scar that went across a two-inch section of his scalp. "I wish I could remember how I got it."

"You will, one of these days! Why, at first you didn't even remember your own name!"

"I'm still not too sure of it, Cookie! But I guess it's Bill Welton, all right!" He shook his head soberly.

"Couldn't be any other!" Cookie insisted. "We found that Wanted notice all folded up real small an' pinned inside your shirt. 'Bill Welton, Wanted for Murder,' it says. 'Six foot tall, light complexion, good talker.' That's you, all right."

Welton nodded glumly. "Some day I'm going to hunt up the U. S. marshal that signed that notice, down on the Border, and get an idea who it was I killed—and how and where."

"While you're at it, find out where you got that rich ore that Deuce picked up alongside you when he found you!" Cookie grinned. "Deuce is sure countin' on getting that half you promised him for saving your life!"

"He'll get it," Welton told him seriously. "I have a feeling it'll all come back to me some day in a rush. And when it does, I'll keep my word to Deuce."

Cookie nodded solemnly. He was sure Welton would. Of all the men who had made Halfway House their temporary home, he liked Welton the best. There was a simple honesty about him that didn't jibe with the shiftiness and out-and-out lawlessness of the others. He didn't seem like a killer, no matter what the Wanted notice said.

"Cookie," the tall young outlaw was saying, "if a man saved your life, would you sit back and let the prison wagon cart him off, when you might be able to stop it?"

"The wagon?" Cookie's fear of the dreaded vehicle was reflected in his voice.

"Gillis says the wagon's due pretty soon in Diablo. Claims they'll have Deuce free before it gets there, but I don't believe it. They've got the envelope, and that's probably all that matters to them."

Cookie nodded. "I'd say you sized Gillis up right. But how you figure to get Deuce out of that jail?"

"I don't know yet. I'll think of something."

Sam Gillis made a point of stopping by the sheriff's office when he got back to town a few hours later.

"Worst fishin' I run into in years," he whined to Luke MacTavish.

Luke was sympathetic but amused. He suspected that Sam had only dropped in to kill time and put off the moment when he would have to face his angry wife at the

hotel. "Did you catch sight of any strangers in the direction of the buttes?" he asked.

"Didn't go that way," Sam lied. "Didn't see a soul out on the trail." He was sitting where he could look right into the cell where Deuce Adams was locked up. "Didn't the posse have any luck?"

"They're still out. I'm waiting to hear." Sheriff Luke hardly got the words out when they heard the sound of hoofbeats out back in the alley behind the jail. "Sounds like them now." He rose and crossed quickly to the door.

The moment the sheriff had hurried out, Sam moved to the cell door. Deuce was waiting, his hand thrust out between the bars. "Hand it over, quick."

"Hand what?" Gillis frowned.

"The gun! The gun! Didn't Chantry send me a gun?"

"Haven't seen him. I been up to the Halfway. Paid off your pardner Welton and got the envelope."

"Good!" Deuce snapped. "Now tell Chantry to get me outa here before the wagon rolls in."

The voices of the sheriff and his deputy, as they came up to the front door from around in the rear of the jail, sent Gillis scurrying back to his chair near the sheriff's desk. "What luck?" he greeted them.

Lofty frowned and brushed the dust off his clothes. "No sign of him."

"Too bad," Sam made a long face. "I suppose now we'll have to wait another couple of months before we can get a new batch of those Texas handbills."

"Maybe not," Luke told him. "I got a telegram off to the Rangers at Austin today. Maybe we can hurry things this time." But he didn't seem too sure of it.

Sam Gillis went on his way to the hotel, chuckling to himself. If that stupid MacTavish and his deputy only knew that he had that missing envelope of theirs right inside his pocket!

He slowed his steps outside the hotel. He was sure he had caught a glimpse of Essie's feather-trimmed hat in there. Then he noticed that there were other feather-trimmed hats as well. And a sound of feminine voices came out the front door, all trying to talk at once, and all apparently in good humor. Something must be going on!

He put on a bold front and went in.

Essie was talking gaily to Sarah Jane Alberts, Miss Murdock the new schoolteacher, and most surprising, Annie Oakley. She looked over their heads and beckoned to him coquettishly. "Sammy dear, come hear the lovely plans we're makin' for a sociable to welcome Miss Murdock to Diablo!"

"Yes, dear!" He saw Tex Chantry open the barroom door and motion with his head, but he couldn't go to him now. Not till Essie had gotten through with him!

"Cake and lemonade" and "Invite all the parents" and "Saturday afternoon at four thirty." The words flew around his head, and he just sat and blinked and nodded approval. When they were all breathless, he said, "That's fine, ladies! You can count on me." But he had no idea what they had been saying, with Chantry scowling impatiently at him from the doorway.

When they left a few minutes later, Essie went with them, sailing out like an ocean liner escorted by a bevy of harbor tugs. He heaved a sigh of relief and hurried to report to Chantry and deliver the envelope for which the gambler had paid two hundred dollars.

Tex saw at once that the wax seals hadn't been broken. He cut them away with his penknife and dumped the folded handbills onto the table in front of him. There were no customers in the barroom to watch him and Gillis, and the bartender was busy at the far end of the bar.

"Now we'll see!" Chantry smoothed out the folded papers. There were at least twenty of the hand-printed reward notices on thin, rough paper. Some had hand-drawn pictures of the wanted man, others were simply the amount of the award and a brief description of him, along with the crimes for which he was wanted.

He thumbed through them rapidly, and down near the bottom of the pile, he found the one for which he had invested his two hundred dollars. "Five Hundred Dollars Reward for the Capture and Conviction of Hamilton Chantry, alias Tex Chantry, Tex Hamilton, etc. Wanted for forgery, petty theft, assault, and highway robbery." It was signed by the sheriff of Kimble County.

"Kimble County!" he smiled. "A great place! I must go back some day!"

Sam Gillis snickered. "Sounds like they'd be glad to see you!"

Chantry laughed. "I'll let them wait." He held up the notice and read it over again, smiling. Then he touched the end of his cigar to it, and watched in silence as the flame crept up, inch by inch, and turned it to black ash. When it was all burned but a tiny piece, he let go of it and dropped it into an ash tray to burn itself away. Then he dumped the ash into the thick sawdust on the floor and kicked it out of sight. "And that's the end of that! Let the wagon come if it wants to!"

Annie and Melinda were on their way home to the ranch. Annie was riding Target, and staying close beside the buggy that Uncle Luke had rented from the livery stable for Melinda to drive back and forth from school during the last weeks of the term.

Melinda had never tried to drive a buggy before, and she was sitting up straight and stiff, hanging onto the reins as if she would never let go.

"That's fine!" Annie called to her, as Melinda guided the horse around an approaching farm wagon.

"It's really not so difficult to drive, is it?" Melinda called back gaily. She giggled. "Wait till Blair finds out I've learned! He always calls me a fraidy cat!"

Annie nodded, smiling, but she was thinking unhappily, "Poor Melinda! I don't know how to tell her!"

There was a copy of a two-month-old *Diablo Gazette* in her saddlebag. It had a story on the front page that would just about break Melinda's heart when Annie could get up the courage to show it to her.

Annie had stopped by the *Gazette* office early that afternoon, just on the chance that Mr. Wiggins, the reporter-editor-publisher combined, might remember some item that he had published during the past two months about a man named Blair Murdock, a prospector.

Mr. Wiggins had been sure at first that he had never heard of anyone named Blair Murdock. But as he said the name over a couple of times, he began to recollect something in connection with it. He waddled into the storeroom in his carpet slippers, and started searching the back files, grumbling and mumbling.

"Can I help?" Annie poked her head around the door.

"If you don't scatter the papers!"

"I'll try not to!" she had promised meekly. And she had been the one who found the item that Mr. Wiggins had faintly remembered printing.

ANOTHER INDIAN OUTRAGE read the column head. And the story, dated two months ago, told how a horse hired from a Bonanza City livery stable by a young man named Blair Murdock, had wandered back to the stable a week after Murdock had ridden it away. Murdock had told the stableman that he was going out to his claim, and had added only that it was near Diablo.

The item related that a search party had tried to back-track to the missing man, but had found no trace of his body. The account closed with the fact that an Indian arrow was still sticking into the cantle of the saddle, and the saddlebags were slashed open and empty. The Bonanza City paper, from which Wiggins had copied the story, had guessed that Indian renegades had killed the prospector and disposed of his body in a remote area of the hills.

"I published it in the *Gazette*," Wiggins told Annie solemnly, "to scare some of these crazy miners into being more careful about riding out alone, like that poor fellow!"

Mr. Wiggins had been very sympathetic about the new schoolteacher's tragedy, and had wanted to get out a special edition of his weekly *Gazette* to tell Diablo all about it. But Annie had persuaded him to wait till Tuesday, the regular publication day. She wanted to break the news to Melinda as gently as possible, before then.

Now, as they rode to the ranch, she still wondered how and when to tell her.

Maybe Uncle Luke would help. He would be home as soon as the town council meeting was over.

When Sheriff Luke finally arrived at the ranch, it was quite late. They had had a stormy session at the council meeting. Doc Busby had wanted to send word to the Governor that a company of militia would be a handy thing to have around, patrolling the roads near the new mining town of Soapstone to protect the miners from the riffraff and criminals who were making them unsafe.

But Sam Gillis had pooh-poohed the idea. He seemed quite sure that when the Tumbleweed Wagon arrived, the badmen would clear out of the neighborhood. Those who didn't would be picked up. One way or another, he argued heatedly, it was a sign of weakness to ask for the militia. The Governor might think they couldn't handle their own affairs. It would be a black eye for Diablo.

There had been a lot of yelling and table-pounding at the meeting, but in the end the council had agreed with Sam Gillis to "wait and see."

Annie met her uncle at the door. She had a cup of hot cocoa waiting for him, and a plateful of cookies, crisp and fresh from the oven.

The tired sheriff stretched his long legs toward the fire and relaxed. "It's good to get home," he said. "No problems here. No arguments and yelling." He had his eyes closed. "No long faces. Just a happy smiling one." He opened one eye suddenly and looked at Annie, sitting a few feet away. "Hey! Where's the smile?"

Annie tried to smile, but it was a sad effort. Her uncle sat up straight. "All right. Out with it. What has Tagg been up to? Another cake of soap in the well?"

Annie shook her head. "Not this time," she told him soberly. "It isn't Tagg. It's this." She handed him the folded newspaper.

He took the paper and read the column quickly. His face was grave as he finished. "How did Melinda take this?"

"I couldn't tell her, Uncle Luke. She's so happy about having the teaching job, I couldn't spoil it. They're even giving a sociable for her Saturday afternoon."

"It does seem a shame," MacTavish admitted. "Maybe no harm would be done if we put off telling her about this till she's had time to get started on her schoolteaching."

"But Mr. Wiggins intends to print the story Tuesday!"

"I think I can get him to hold it back another week," Sheriff Luke said soberly. "It isn't as if they had found Murdock's body. He still might show up!"

"That's right, Uncle Luke! So he might!"

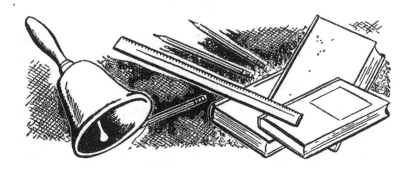

8 The Sociable

Saturday morning started off busily for a lot of people in and around the little desert town of Diablo.

In many a home the lady of the house was up before daylight, mixing up and baking her most prized cake for the sociable late that afternoon at the schoolhouse. And many a man of the house was rousted out of bed an hour earlier than usual, to carry in extra wood for the range, and to get busy cutting a small boy's hair so he would look less like a savage when he met his new teacher for the first time.

The guest of honor woke early and blinked at the bright sun streaming in through her window. She sat up smiling. Then she leaned over and tapped on Annie's wall. They had agreed that whoever woke up first, every morning, would tap and wake the other.

But there was no answering tap from Annie's side, and after trying it again, she hopped out of bed and ran to the door and opened it to listen. Sure enough, she heard Annie's voice down in the kitchen, and the sheriff's deep one. She decided to surprise them by getting dressed in a hurry and popping in on them. She was usually a sleepy-head, but today she felt excited and happy.

"Honey," Sheriff Luke was telling his niece, across the pine table set for breakfast, "the best way to tell Melinda, when you do, is straight out. Show her that clipping, but tell her it may not be as bad as it sounds. Lots of men are lost for weeks, and come through all right."

"Well, at least poor Melinda will have a few happy days before we tell her," Annie said with a sigh.

"Tell me what?" Melinda, her eyes wide and startled, stared at them from the hall door. "What's wrong? Is it—Blair?"

Annie moved quickly to her and took her hand to draw her over to a chair. "I'm afraid so," she said honestly. "We didn't want to tell you just yet, but there's been some news that—that might be bad."

"Nothing proved," Sheriff Luke said hastily, as he held a chair for her at the table. "Annie found an item in an old *Gazette* that could mean he'd had an accident—"

"An accident? He's been hurt, hasn't he? Where is he?" She looked from one to the other in alarm.

"We don't know any more than it tells us here, Miss Melinda," the sheriff said gently, holding out the newspaper to her, "but I aim to find out all I can about it."

Melinda read the story hastily and then cried a little on Annie's shoulder. After a while, they talked over whether Sheriff Luke should call off the party in Melinda's honor this afternoon.

"Please don't," she said finally. "And please don't tell anybody about this yet. After all," she smiled bravely, "we have no proof that Blair was—was killed by Indians. Maybe he was somewhere else when the Indians shot at his horse and cut open the saddlebags. He could have been inside the tunnel at his claim."

"That's right, Uncle Luke!" Annie added excitedly. "And maybe he's stranded out there, because he hasn't a horse to ride into town! That could be, couldn't it?"

"It certainly could!" her uncle assured her, "and Lofty and I will both try to find him as soon as we can."

Melinda smiled through her tears. "I know you will!"

"And we won't say a word about it today!"

"That's good," Melinda sighed. "I don't think I could stand all the talking there'd be about it, even though everyone would be sympathetic!"

"We'll tell them after Uncle Luke brings your brother back safely!" Annie promised, with a firm belief that her uncle couldn't fail.

It was almost noon when Chet Alberts and a couple of other husbands finished decorating the schoolroom with the bunting Chet had brought over from the Emporium. He had also donated the use of the long planks that were going to be used for tables when the ladies brought in the refreshments late in the afternoon.

Tagg had ridden into town alongside the sheriff early in the morning. Annie had made him wear his Sunday suit and his shined-up shoes, but he had changed to overalls as soon as they arrived, so he could help to get the schoolroom ready for the sociable.

He had been busy hammering tacks in the rough-finished log walls, to hold up the bunting, when Mrs. Essie Gillis had come up the walk looking for him. She was carrying a sheet of writing paper in her hand, and Tagg heard her tell Chet Alberts that it was a poem of welcome she had

written in Miss Murdock's honor, and she was looking for
Tagg Oakley to recite it this evening.

Tagg had stooped down and tried to make a quick exit
by the side door, before she could find him. But as luck
would have it, he had run smack into Chick Bergen, the
livery stable man, carrying a plank. Chick had dropped the
plank with a crash that brought Chet Alberts and everyone
else running to investigate, and Mrs. Gillis had pounced
on Tagg.

Tagg had tried to talk himself out of reciting the poem,
but Mrs. Gillis had been determined. "Your uncle's always
talkin' so big about how smart you an' that sister of yours
are. Now you'll get a chance to show off!"

"But it sounds silly!" Tagg scowled, glancing at the
paper.

The stout woman's lips had tightened into a straight line
and she had said angrily, "You do like I tell you. That's
a good poem an' you're a sassy little boy. You'll learn it for
the party, or I'll see that your uncle gives you a good
larrupin'!"

"Uncle Luke never larrups me!"

"If he don't, he oughta!" she had flung at him. "And
that gun-totin' sister of yours needs some, too!"

Tagg had to swallow hard to keep from talking back to her, but he had managed it somehow. Annie had told him a lot of times never to be impudent to his elders, no matter how mad they made him. But Mrs. Gillis almost made him forget.

"See that you don't make any mistakes!" she had warned him before she flounced away.

He had gone around in back of the schoolhouse, under the shade of the cottonwood in the playground, and tried honestly to learn the poem. It was just plain terrible, he knew. But she was head of the school board, and he didn't want her to get mad and maybe take out her spite on Miss Murdock because Miss Murdock lived at their ranch.

"To the lady who has come from far away," he had that much by heart, "We are gathered to say howdy here today!" Ugh! He put the paper down beside him and leaned back against the tree.

A gentle breeze was shaking the cottonwood and making a soothing soft sound. His eyes felt heavy. Inside the schoolroom, the men had stopped hammering and all he could hear was a low hum of voices. Before he knew it, he was sound asleep.

When he woke up, buggy wheels were rolling into the

schoolyard, and there was a gay clatter of dishes and conversation from the schoolroom.

He sat up quickly and looked around him in a daze. From the position of the sun, it must be mighty close to three o'clock or after. He hadn't much time to learn the rest of that silly jingle that Mrs. Gillis called a poem. He yawned and reached out his hand for it.

But the piece of writing paper with the poem scribbled on it was gone.

He was startled wide-awake. He looked around him hastily, but there was no sign of the paper. His heart sank. Mrs. Gillis would never believe he hadn't lost it purposely!

Then he saw Chick Bergen's small white and black puppy chewing something, over by the steps. The something looked very much like a piece of paper.

He ran over quickly and succeeded in getting what was left of the paper away from the puppy, after a struggle that the puppy enjoyed heartily. It was the poem, right enough, or what was left of it—part of the first two lines.

"Well, now I don't have to learn it, and it isn't my fault," he told himself cheerfully. Tagg was never one to argue with Lady Luck.

He patted the small puppy and went whistling up the steps to find out how long it would be before the party started.

At the ranch house, Annie and Melinda were almost ready to leave for the schoolhouse.

"Are you sure you feel like going?" Annie asked gently.

"I'll be all right, thank you," Melinda sighed, "but I'll be glad when it's over."

Annie stood off to look her over approvingly. "You look lovely in that blue dress. Only you're so pale they'll notice, I'm afraid."

Melinda gave herself a quick look, and then pinched her cheeks till they were pink and glowing.

"That's better!" Annie smiled. She was wearing the same sort of riding outfit that she usually did, except that the blouse was of the finest white satin, instead of denim, and the fringed white leather vest was decorated with handsome silver disks called conchas. Her divided riding skirt was white doeskin with long fringe trimming, and her boots were decorated with leather carving that wove her initials into a circle crossed by the outline of a rifle.

"I feel sort of silly, all dressed up," she confided to

Melinda, "but Uncle Luke spent a lot of money on this dude-y outfit, and I want to show it off to please him!"

"It's lovely!" Melinda said quickly. "It just suits you!"

They were getting into the buggy a few minutes later when Melinda noticed that Annie wasn't wearing her familiar gun belt and Colt revolver.

"Thank goodness!" Melinda said frankly. "I hate the sight of guns. I wonder if I'll ever get used to them!"

"I hope the time'll come when nobody out here has to wear them," Annie said solemnly, "but we have a long time to go before that, I'm afraid!"

The tall man who thought his name must be Bill Welton was riding down the long hot trail from the Black Buttes. He wore two six-shooters, one for Deuce Adams and one for himself. He rode a horse that Cookie had lent him, and led a second for Deuce Adams. And he moved slowly, because he didn't want to get into Diablo till dusk.

Annie stopped the buggy outside the sheriff's office, and Lofty strode out into the street to greet the girls.

He was all slicked up and wearing a bright blue tie that Annie noticed was just the color of Melinda's eyes. She

held back a grin as he swept off his hat and made a bow
to them. "You're lookin' right pretty, ladies," he said.

"Why, thank you," Melinda said, blushing.

"Hi, where's Uncle?" Annie asked.

"Finishing a checker game with Doc Busby," Lofty
answered, but his eyes still rested on Melinda, whose cheeks
stayed pink under his admiring gaze.

"Guess I better dig him out," Annie said cheerfully.
"Would you mind driving Melinda down to the school?
If you're not busy?"

"Not doin' a thing!" he assured her quickly, and was in
the buggy and starting off with a flourish before she could
catch her breath.

Annie laughed and ran on into the office. She didn't
think Lofty would make as much of an impression on the
eastern young lady as he hoped, but his admiration might
take Melinda's mind off her brother, for a little while
anyhow.

Uncle Luke and Doc Busby were deep in their checker
game when Annie came in, and they didn't even look up.
She glanced back toward Deuce Adams' cell, and saw the
sullen prisoner staring out at her with a sour expression.

"Three good meals a day," she thought grimly, "and

a good place to sleep. He doesn't know how lucky he is now, but wait till the Tumbleweed Wagon gets here and he starts working for his keep!"

Doc Busby slapped a checker on the board and chortled gleefully, "I'll jump this—an' this—an' there you are!"

Sheriff Luke scratched his ear and sighed. "Looks like you got me that time! But the next one'll be different!"

Annie put her hands down on the board and leaned on them, grinning at her uncle. "No next one! You promised to be at the sociable on time, and you're late now!"

"Go ahead, Luke," Doc grinned, "let the ladies see you're supportin' culture 'an' refinement in the mee-tropolis of Diablo!"

Annie handed her uncle his hat and waited. He rose with a sigh of resignation. "All right. But I'll be back an' lick the daylights out of you in a few minutes."

Doc chuckled. "That'll be a snowy day in July!" he said, and winked at Annie.

Sheriff Luke stopped in the doorway as Annie went out ahead of him. "I'll set the spring lock, so nobody wanders in while I'm gone."

Doc grinned and waved him on. He had started to lay out a solitaire game with an old pack of playing cards.

Luke could lock the door or not, as he saw fit. Doc never worried about what might happen. "We'll take care of it when it comes," was his comfortable philosophy.

Sheriff Luke and Annie could see that the schoolhouse was already filled with grownups and children, with more arriving all the time. The chatter and laughter came in a steady stream through the open windows and doors.

"They won't miss me if I don't go in," he objected, but Annie held onto his arm and steered him up to the front door.

Inside, Annie saw Mrs. Gillis move majestically up onto the teacher's platform where Melinda was sitting with her hands folded in her lap, trying to smile but only succeeding in looking nervous and worried.

"And now," Mrs. Gillis boomed, "we'll have our poem of welcome that I wrote myself. Master Tagg Oakley will give the recitation."

"Come on, let's hurry! Tagg's going to recite!" Annie pulled her uncle in past the men who were grouped, lounging, on the school steps. "I didn't know it! He and Mrs. Gillis must have planned it as a surprise!"

Tagg, seated against the wall with half a dozen of his schoolmates, gave a gasp. He had clean forgotten to tell

Mrs. Gillis what had happened to her poem!

He jumped up and started to streak for the door, but Chick Bergen was too quick for him. With a laugh he grabbed the runaway by the sleeve and hauled him up to the platform.

Tagg stood there staring transfixed at the sea of eyes. He opened his mouth to speak, but no sound came out. He tried again. This time he brought out, "Ladies—" but his voice broke into a squeak, and some of the men standing out on the steps laughed.

Tagg's face got red, and he clenched his fists and started over again. "Ladies—" and his voice failed him once more.

"How about the gents?" came a voice from outside.

On the platform, Mrs. Sam Gillis leaned over and hit Tagg sharply on the shoulder with her palm-leaf fan. "Go on! 'Ladies and gentlemen'—what's the matter? Don't be so stupid!"

"Ladies and gentlemen, what's the matter? Don't be so stupid!" Tagg blurted out. Then, as the audience broke into a roar of laughter, he gave them a stricken look and bolted off the platform and out the side door into the late afternoon dusk.

9 Captured

Mrs. Gillis was furious. The whole roomful of people were laughing at Tagg for getting her poem all mixed up. "I bet he did it a-purpose," she said angrily to Melinda. Then she got up and hammered on the desk with her fist. "Ladies and gentlemen!" But they kept laughing, and she had an idea that they were laughing at her as well as Tagg.

Annie wanted to rush up to the platform and tell everyone what she thought of them for making fun of Tagg, but Uncle Luke held her back. "Forget it, honey," he said hastily, "it's only natural for folks to laugh. If it was anybody but Tagg, you'd see the funny side, too!"

"I suppose you're right," Annie admitted. She turned and started toward the door. "I'm going to find him. There's no reason for him to miss the ice cream and lemonade."

She slipped out the side door while Mrs. Gillis was in the midst of reciting her own welcome poem. Nobody wanted to hear it, but they had to now, or hurt her feelings.

Annie couldn't be sure which way Tagg had run, but she felt sure it would be in the direction of the sheriff's office where Pixie was tied in the shed alongside her uncle's horse, Chief. The poor little fellow would be in a hurry to start for home without waiting for her and Uncle Luke.

She hurried down the nearly deserted sidewalk toward the office. She noticed that Doc had pulled down the window shade but a narrow strip of light was showing below the shade. There were very few other lights burning in any other buildings.

She hoped that Tagg was inside with Doc. She knew Doc would sympathize and make him feel better.

Then, as she crossed the side street half a block away from the jail, she stopped suddenly and stared at the tall figure of a man that had come around the corner of the jail and was moving toward the front door, keeping suspiciously close to the building. She caught a glint of reflected light on something in his hand. It was undoubtedly a gun.

She reached quickly for her own six-shooter, only to recollect that tonight she wasn't wearing a gun belt. All

she could do was to step quickly into the shadow of a doorway, and watch to see what the man was up to. She thought
she could guess!

Now he was at the front door and was reaching out to
turn the doorknob, his gun held ready in his other hand.
Annie was relieved when she saw that the door didn't open
when he tried it. She was glad Uncle Luke had set the
spring lock before they left for the party.

The intruder seemed baffled for a moment. Then he
dropped his gun into its holster and went to the window.
He squatted down and looked into the office through the
six-inch space between the shade and the window sill.

Annie saw his face plainly as the lamplight shone on it.
He was the ambusher who had robbed the stage with Deuce
Adams!

She looked around desperately for a weapon, something
—anything—she could use. But there wasn't even a loose
stone or a chunk of wood that she could throw at the
gunman.

She saw something else, though, that almost made her
heart stop. Another shadow was coming around the corner
of the very store in whose doorway she was crouching!

For a bad moment, she thought it was another gunslinger.

Then she realized that it was a very short shadow, and had a familiar outline.

Tagg came slowly around the corner and onto the sidewalk. He was shuffling along, head down, apparently on his way to the sheriff's office. He was going to run smack into the gunman.

Annie reached out and grabbed his sleeve. As he opened his mouth to yell, she clapped her hand over it and yanked him into the doorway beside her.

"Sh-h-h!" she hissed into his ear. "Don't move!"

Tagg didn't. He knew Annie wouldn't be playing games.

After a moment, she cautiously stuck her head out of the doorway to see what was going on at the office. The tall bandit was boldly knocking on the door now. His gun was still in its holster. They could hear him call out, "I have a telegram for Sheriff MacTavish."

There was a pause, during which she wished she could call out a warning to Doc Busby not to open the door, but with Tagg beside her she didn't dare risk startling the gunman and perhaps making him open fire at her.

"Quick!" she whispered. "Go back to the school and tell Uncle Luke! It looks like a jail break!"

But Tagg held back. "You go with me! You don't have

your gun! You can't do anything alone to stop him!"

"Please go, Tagg! Hurry! Maybe I'll think of something!"·

She gave him a little push, and he hurried away around the corner of the building. She felt very much alone and a little frightened for an instant. Then, as she saw Doc open the office door and the tall man whip out his gun and push Doc inside, she forgot to be frightened. She had to do something.

She stepped off the sidewalk and ran down the street to the office. A quick glance through the uncovered part of the window showed her that Doc, sitting down again, with his hands up, was safe for the moment. The tall bandit still held the gun, but he was relaxed now and even smiling at Doc, who was taking it all very calmly as usual.

She thought, "Wonder where he left his horse?" and the idea came to her how she might interfere with the jail break. There were probably two horses waiting. . . .

Annie ran around the corner into the alley and back to the rear of the jail, making as little noise as possible on the way.

The only horses tied in the jail shed were Uncle Luke's big roan Chief and Tagg's little pony Pixie.

She could see moving shadows darkening the high window of one jail cell, and guessed that the bandit was releasing Deuce Adams. In a minute or two, they should be coming hurriedly this way to get to their horses. The gunman *must* have tied them close by! But where?

Then she had the answer. A horse snorted just a few feet away and kicked the boards of the shed.

She ran around to the back of the shed, and there they were, two of them. One was the very critter she had ridden when she tried to catch the ambusher!

She went to the first horse and started hastily to unbuckle the girth strap that held the saddle in place. It was tight, and she had to struggle to open the buckle, but she finally managed to loosen it just enough to leave the saddle apparently safely anchored to the horse.

Then she hurried to the second animal and did the same thing.

Now she could hear the crunch of footsteps in the alley and the low voices of the two men as they came hurriedly toward the shed.

She jumped into the dark shadows on the far side of the shed, looking around her desperately for something she could use as a weapon.

She saw the men hurry to their horses and start to untie them. At the same time, she heard a commotion and loud voices from the direction of the schoolhouse. Evidently Tagg had reached Uncle Luke with news of the jail break.

The men heard, too. Both started a quick mount, but the moment each had his left foot in the stirrup, his saddle started to slip and turn. Both grabbed wildly and tried to stay upright, but it was no use. Over went the saddles, out of them went the men, and away went the frightened, squealing, bucking horses.

As the two men, bruised and confused, scrambled to their feet, they heard Annie sing out, "Up with your hands!" They knew that voice, and when they turned to see where she was, they saw her standing in the shadow, with a short thick something in her hand that they were sure was her Colt .45.

They had seen her in action with that six gun, so they had no disposition to defy her. Up went their hands.

And that was the tableau that Luke and Deputy Lofty saw as they ran in with drawn guns.

It took only a second for Lofty to relieve the pair of their guns and replace them with handcuffs.

"Good for you, Annie!" her uncle called out. And it

was only then that Annie stepped out of the shadow and the two angry outlaws discovered that the ".45" in her hand had been only a short length of wood and not her revolver.

By this time, quite a few people had hurried in to see what was going on. Sam Gillis was among them, well up in the forefront of the crowd. He stayed there to congratulate Annie, and then slipped away to report to Tex Chantry that Bill Welton hadn't waited for them to release Deuce Adams, but had tried to do it himself, and Annie Oakley had cornered them both with a bluff.

Outside the front of the jail, Mrs. Gillis had brought Melinda to see the excitement. Melinda hadn't wanted to come, but Mrs. Gillis had suggested that it would look friendlier to Diablo if the new schoolteacher joined in with the rest of the folks and showed an interest. So Melinda had had to let herself be steered here.

Now she found herself near the front of the crowd with Mrs. Gillis as Sheriff Luke and Lofty marched the two handcuffed men up the steps toward the open office door. Melinda saw both their faces distinctly in the lamplight.

She stared, stunned, at the face of the tall man. It was her brother Blair! Instead of lying dead out in some lonely desert spot, or working alone on his claim in the hills, her brother was an outlaw caught in the act of trying to free his partner in crime!

It came back to her in a flash that there had seemed to be something familiar about him at the stage holdup, in spite of his disguise. She had put the thought away at once, but now she knew that she had really recognized him then.

Her head spun and she had to clutch Mrs. Gillis' arm to keep from collapsing. The stout woman looked at her with surprise. "What are you scared about?" she asked bluntly. "They're handcuffed!"

"He—that man—" Melinda gasped, "he's—"

"You mean *you know him?*" Mrs. Gillis was shocked.

Annie had joined them. She laughed. "I should say she does know him! Several of us do! It's that slippery ambusher who got away at the stage holdup!"

Mrs. Gillis relaxed. "Oh, I see! No wonder it gave you a bad turn to look at his ugly face!" She patted Melinda's shoulder.

Melinda managed to smile. She was grateful that Annie had accidentally interrupted just when she did. Melinda had been on the verge of telling Mrs. Gillis that the outlaw was Blair! That would have been the end of her school job, she felt sure. And she needed it desperately now, more than ever.

Mrs. Gillis smiled apologetically, "I mighta known a real lady like *you* wouldn't be friend to an *outlaw!* But you never know about people these days."

She took Melinda by the arm and started to lead her back to the school. Melinda looked at Annie, half tempted to excuse herself and tell her friend the truth. But Annie had turned away and gone into the office after her uncle and Lofty and the prisoners. So Melinda obediently went back to the sociable and smiled and tried to be cheerful and friendly to her future pupils' parents.

Inside the sheriff's office, Doc Busby was sputtering indignantly and rubbing his chafed wrists. "I was just about to beat that solitaire game when that long-legged coyote barged in the door with his gun and in the hooraw all the cards got mixed up! I reckon I'll never get that close again to winning!"

He wouldn't even stay for a last checker game with Luke, nor let Annie coax him into coming down to the school for refreshments. He climbed into his rickety buggy, chirruped to his old sorrel mare, Miss Lightnin', and went on home, still muttering and shaking his head.

In adjoining cells, Deuce Adams and Bill Welton lay down on their cots and turned their backs to the lamplight on Sheriff Luke's desk.

Deuce was soon snoring. He was still sure Tex Chantry would get him and Bill Welton out in plenty of time to escape the Tumbleweed Wagon. Too bad that Welton had made a fizzle of his jail break and been caught himself. But it was not all to the bad, he thought just as he dropped off to sleep. For now Welton was right here with him, and if the big fellow suddenly recollected just where it was that he had dug out that rich ore, Deuce would be close by to see that nobody else cheated him out of the half share Welton had promised him!

But Welton wasn't trying to remember just then. He was lying awake thinking bitterly of how he had failed to free his friend. Now they would have to depend on Sam Gillis and Tex Chantry, and he didn't have much faith in either of them.

Down the street, Melinda was smiling as she told Lofty how glad she was that the robbers had been captured. But behind the smile she was thinking desperately, "I *must* get to Blair somehow and find out what all this is about!"

10   The Girl at the Window

It was only a little after ten o'clock when the sociable ended and the guests set out for their homes, some of them in town and others at a distance. Everyone said it had been a very nice party, and they all felt that the school board had made a good choice, picking out Miss Murdock to teach their children. She was most certainly a lady.

Annie noticed as she and Melinda drove home together that the girl seemed very tired and thoughtful. She thought Melinda was worrying about her brother's disappearance. It was only natural, and Annie felt that it wouldn't help to start talking about it.

When they got to the house, Melinda excused herself almost right away to go to her room. She had a very bad headache, she told Annie, and sleep was the only thing that would help it.

Annie saw Tagg safely into bed, and then went down to the living room to wait for Uncle Luke to come in from putting away Chief and Pixie. Tagg had been just too sleepy to do his usual job of settling the little pony for the night, and Uncle Luke had good-naturedly agreed to do it for him this once.

Behind her closed bedroom door, Melinda had stood listening tensely as Annie went by from Tagg's room and down the stairs. When she was sure that she had heard her busy with the fire in the fireplace, moving the logs that had been smouldering all evening behind the iron screen, Melinda opened her door very quietly and stepped into the hall.

But she didn't go downstairs. Instead she tiptoed to Annie's bedroom door, a few feet away, and opened it. For a moment she listened nervously to the sounds downstairs. Luke was coming in, and Annie was telling him that she would be glad to make him some tea if he'd like it. When Melinda heard Luke say it would taste right good, she knew that she would not be disturbed for several minutes. She slipped into the bedroom, but left the door open.

In a couple of minutes she came out quickly, carrying some of Annie's clothing over her arm, and holding a pair of Annie's older riding boots in her hand. She closed the door noiselessly and tiptoed back into her own room.

Annie and her Uncle Luke had gone into the kitchen to brew his tea. When Annie had put on the teakettle, the sheriff suggested, "Maybe you better run up and see if Melinda would like some hot tea for her headache."

"That's a good idea, Uncle Luke. I never thought of it! I'll go right up."

She hurried up the stairs to Melinda's room and tapped lightly on the door. For a moment there was no answer. Then Melinda's voice answered faintly, "Yes?"

"Oh, I'm sorry if you were asleep! I just wanted to know if you'd like some tea for your headache."

On the other side of the door, Melinda stood in the dark, fully dressed in Annie's old riding outfit, boots, and hat. "No, thank you," she made her voice sound sleepy. "I'll be all right as soon as I have some sleep."

"Okay, then. But if there's anything I can do for you during the night, don't hold back. Just bang on the wall, or if I don't hear you, come right in and wake me."

"I will, thank you," Melinda answered sleepily. A minute later she heard Annie go down the stairs and into the kitchen and close the door behind her. "I hope they don't sit around down there too long," she thought fretfully. "I want to get to town and back before daylight."

It seemed like an hour to her, but it was only twenty minutes later that she heard Annie call out, "Good night, Uncle Luke!" down in the kitchen, and guessed that the sheriff had gone to his bedroom, which was in the rear of the house just off the kitchen.

Then she heard Annie come up the stairs and go into her room, closing the door softly.

For a moment, Melinda almost decided to go to Annie right then and tell her about Blair. Then she stopped herself. She knew Annie would be surprised, and very sympathetic. But, after all, Annie was the sheriff's niece and she might think it was right to tell him who the outlaw really was. And if Sheriff MacTavish knew, others would have to know, and it would get to Mrs. Gillis. And that would be the end of Melinda in Diablo. She would be cast out in disgrace, with no way of making a living!

So she couldn't tell Annie, even though she wante '

In a few minutes the house was very still. Downstairs big grandfather clock in the living room struck twelve, and every stroke made her heart jump. When the striking stopped, she slipped out into the hall and down the stairway, carrying Annie's boots, slipping along like a shadow.

She was glad the stairs didn't creak! And a few minutes later, as she shut the kitchen door behind her, she was glad that the door hinges were well oiled and didn't betray her by squeaking.

She opened the barn doors carefully and went in. Moonlight was streaming through the doorway, and she didn't have to light the lantern to see. She went first to Target's stall, but when she reached out to touch Annie's horse he backed away from her, tossing his head, stamping and snorting, and baring his teeth. She moved away hastily to Chief, Sheriff Luke's horse. Chief stood still while she patted him, and came along peaceably when she led him out and awkwardly started to saddle him.

She had saddled horses before, at finishing school, but the saddles were different. She fumbled a little, and took more time than she wanted to, but she finally got it adjusted firmly on Chief's back.

She was a little nervous about riding on the unfamiliar western saddle, but she was too desperate to let it stop her. She mounted and rode out, making as little noise as possible, keeping Chief at a walk till they were out of sight of the house, with the barn between.

Then she rode as swiftly as she dared on the road to Diablo.

Bill Welton sat up suddenly on the cot in his cell. He looked up at the slitted, barred window, and saw that the sky was still dark. He wondered what had jolted him awake, and he swung his feet to the packed-down dirt floor and stood beside his cot, listening.

Deuce was snoring in the next cell, and his snores kept on steadily. Welton went to his door and peered through the bars toward the front office.

The kerosene lamp on the desk was still burning. By its faint light, he saw the tall young deputy's legs stretched out across the top of the desk, one foot crossed over the other. The feet didn't move while Welton watched them. He guessed that the deputy was sound asleep.

He had almost decided that it was one of Deuce's louder snores which had awakened him, when he heard a sound out back in the direction of the alley.

He moved quickly to his cell window and looked out. The sound came again. It was the noise of a horse shaking its bridled head. And since he knew that the Deputy's own horse was tied in front at the hitch rack, and the two

horses which he had brought down in his luckless attempt
to rescue Deuce had run off, he decided hopefully that Tex
Chantry had sent someone to break them out of jail. "Deuce
was right!" he thought with relief. "I didn't give Chantry
credit!"

When his eyes had become used to the darkness, he saw
a movement out there in the shadows. He tried to make
out how many horses they had brought, and was surprised
and a bit alarmed to see the outline of only one.

He was even more surprised when a figure emerged from
the shadows and moved into the moonlight. It was a girl in
a fringed jacket and skirt. It looked familiar. It looked
like nobody but Annie Oakley. The outfit was the same as
she always wore, and the size was the same. But what was
the sheriff's niece doing, sneaking around outside the rear
of his jail at this hour of the night?

He was amazed to see her pick up a small empty crate
from a pile of trash and bring it toward the cell window.
He drew back into the darkness of the cell and waited.

He heard her step up onto the box, and a moment later
he saw her head block the small square of window. He
couldn't see her face.

She spoke in a soft whisper. "Blair! Blair dear! It's

Linny! Are you in there?" Her eyes probed the darkness.

Welton looked surprised. That wasn't Annie Oakley! It was somebody wearing the same kind of clothing, but it wasn't the sheriff's niece. It was somebody who had made a mistake about who was in the cell.

He moved into the moonlight so she could see his face. Then, in a whisper, so he wouldn't wake up Deuce or the deputy, he said, "I'm sorry, little lady, but there's nobody called Blair in here. You have the wrong jail, I'm afraid!"

"Blair!" she sounded a little angry. "Don't stand there and say things like that! I came a long way to see you, and I'm taking an awful risk!"

"Sorry, my dear," he said good-humoredly, still keeping his voice low, "but my name is Bill Welton, and I don't know who you are!"

"Oh, Blair, what's happened to you?" She was frightened and tearful now and her voice rose sharply above the whisper in which she tried to keep it. "Why didn't you come to Diablo to get my telegram? Why are you pretending to be an outlaw?"

He was impatient now. He knew she would have both the deputy and Deuce awake in another minute. "You have the wrong man, miss. I tell you, I don't know you and you don't know me. And you'd better go away at once, before you wake up somebody and start a big hullabaloo!"

"Hey!" It was Deuce's voice, low and harsh. "You talkin' in your sleep there, Bill?"

"Go away, quickly, miss!" Welton whispered to the girl.

She moved back hastily and disappeared from the window. But a second later, he heard a small crash and an exclamation of distress, and guessed rightly that she had tipped over the crate and had a tumble.

Then he heard the deputy's boots hit the floor up front in the office, and a moment later saw him stride up to the cell door. "What's the racket here?" He peered in, still only half awake and very much annoyed.

Before Welton could speak, Deuce called out cheerfully, "Aw, go back to sleep, lawman! You been dreamin'!"

But all three of them could hear the sound of light, running footsteps out in back of the jail. Deputy Lofty wheeled and ran out the front door, grabbing up his gun belt and buckling it on as he went.

Melinda had picked herself up after her unlucky tumble and run to her horse. Her hands trembled as she hurriedly untied Chief from the rail inside the shed. She must get away before anyone recognized her.

Now she had the horse free, and even as Lofty's steps
rang on the wooden walk beside the jail, she settled in the
saddle and started the big horse toward the alley.

Lofty dashed around the corner of the building in time
to see the girl in Annie's familiar riding outfit disappear
at a canter into the darkness of the alley.

He came to an abrupt stop and stood staring after her in
amazement. Annie Oakley sneaking around the rear of
the jail long past midnight! It just couldn't be.

Deuce was standing on his cot, peering out the high
cell window. He watched the deputy staring after the disappearing girl. Then he saw him turn and come back toward
the jail, head down, moving slowly.

Deuce jumped off his cot and strode to the cell door.
"Bill," he spoke softly, "how many guns did Chantry send
us? Where's mine? Quick!"

Bill Welton came close to his own door. "She didn't come
from Chantry. The poor thing was looking for someone she
called Blair. Probably her husband."

"Blair?" Deuce scowled. "Never heard of him!"

Lofty's heavy steps crossed the office floor. He stood in
front of the cells and glared at the two men. "What did
Miss Oakley want? Which one of you did she talk to?"

Bill Welton answered promptly, "That wasn't—"

Deuce laughed roughly before Bill Welton could continue. "Don't tell him, Bill! Let him suffer!" the older outlaw jeered. "If she wanted you to know anything, she'da told you!" He saw Lofty's face darken with anger, and he laughed again and snapped his fingers in the deputy's face.

"I've got a good mind to come in there and knock the truth out of you!" Lofty raged. "What did she want?"

"Now, now, little man!" Deuce laughed. "Miss Oakley wouldn't like you to talk that way to her friends!"

Lofty stood for a moment with his hands clenched and then turned on his heel and stalked into the office. After a moment he went out and stood on the front step and stared blackly into the empty street. He could hear the hoofbeats of a lone horse dying away far down the street. He hadn't any doubt that it was Annie's horse that he heard, and he would have followed her fast if there had been anyone he could have left to guard the two prisoners.

Bill Welton spoke quietly to the man in the next cell. "You know that girl wasn't Annie Oakley! What's the idea of letting him think so?"

Deuce snickered. "Just thought I'd stir up a little trouble for Miss Sharpshooter. I figger we owe it to her!"

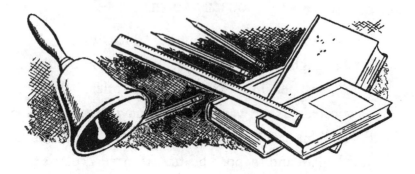

11   A Promise Made

The main street of Diablo was all but deserted, although there were still sounds of Saturday night celebration in some of the houses that Melinda passed as she directed her horse toward the desert road.

At the edge of town, the houses of the respectable residents, sitting behind their small squares of lawn and flowers, stood dark and silent, aloof from the rowdy town. The last lamp had been turned out, the last door locked.

It was a good thing for Melinda's peace of mind that she was unable to see past the lace curtains that moved gently in the desert breeze at Mrs. Sam Gillis' second-story bedroom window. Because Mrs. Gillis was sitting there in the dark, watching her ride by.

Essie had had one of her stomach upsets, which was a polite way of saying that she had, as usual, stuffed herself with too many goodies at the sociable, and now she couldn't sleep. She had been sitting up in her rocking chair by the window, waiting till the memory of that third piece of chocolate layer cake faded.

She had been just about to go to bed when she had heard the hoofbeats of a fast-moving horse coming up the street. Peering out hastily, she saw that the rider was a girl. At second glance she recognized Annie's familiar riding outfit.

Like Lofty Craig, only a few minutes before, she was positive that the rider could be no one but Annie Oakley.

She thought spitefully, "Why, the sly thing! Riding around alone at this time of night! I bet she's been up to something she's ashamed of, or she wouldn't be in such a hurry to leave town."

She pulled the curtains aside so she could lean far out the window and watch the slim figure on the horse disappear into the blackness of the desert road.

Then she sat back and smiled with satisfaction at the thought of the nice bit of gossip she would be able to retail to her friends tomorrow after church.

It was some time later that Annie woke with a start and sat up in bed wondering what had awakened her. She located the sound at once. Someone was turning the door knob, which had a persistent little squeak she had never been able to locate with the oil can.

Her hand groped for the strip of sulphur matches that she kept on the little table beside her bed. She lit one and held it up over her head as she looked toward the opening door. She couldn't see who was coming in, but she decided it must be Melinda looking for something for that mean headache she had complained of earlier. She said quietly, "Hello, there! Come on in!"

But it was Tagg who entered and came over to her, speaking with a little quaver in his voice. "Annie," he said, "somethin' is going on in the barn."

Annie listened a moment, letting the sulphur match burn down. There was no sound through her open window. "Can't hear a thing, hon," she assured him. "Maybe you dreamed it."

"No, I didn't." He sounded a little hurt. "I heard one of the horses kickin' a while ago," he whispered. "And I looked out just now, and both the barn doors were standing wide open!"

Annie patted his shoulder. "Uncle Luke probably forgot to close them, and the horses didn't like the bright moon-

light streaming in. Maybe it was keeping them awake."
She laughed softly. "I'd better tend to it."

"Maybe a bobcat's around or a coyote," he said hopefully. "Can I go along?"

"Indeed not, young feller! You trot right back to bed before you catch cold. I'll stop by when I come in and tell you all about it."

"Okay." Tagg yawned sleepily in spite of trying to hold it back. "But I won't be able to get to sleep till you do."

She slipped out of bed and put on a heavy robe and slippers. On her way to the head of the stairs she stopped a second outside Melinda's room, but there was no sound. "Good!" she thought. "Tagg didn't wake her up, prowling around. I hope she got over her headache."

She picked up a lantern and some matches in the kitchen, and started across the back yard toward the barn, moving quietly and keeping as much as possible in the deep blue shadows. By the bright moonlight, she could see that Tagg had been right about the barn doors being wide open. It was strange. Uncle Luke was usually very careful about closing them tight.

She had brought her rifle along in case she ran into one of those bobcats Tagg had mentioned. Sometimes they could be fighty if you cornered them accidentally. She shuffled her feet as she went into the barn, hoping the critter, if there was one, would scoot out and away without an argument.

Everything in the barn seemed quite peaceful. Her pet, Target, stuck his handsome head out of the stall and nickered a soft greeting to her as she came up to him and gave him a little scratch between the ears. Then she went on to take a quick look at the other horses.

She saw at once that Chief's stall was empty and his saddle was gone.

She knew her uncle hadn't ridden him away, because when she had passed his door a few minutes ago she had heard his regular deep breathing.

Someone—probably some passing tumbleweed of a cowboy—had gone into the sheriff's barn and stolen Chief. It must have been when Tagg heard the horse stamping.

She noticed a slender boot print in the dirt floor of Chief's stall. She knelt and held the lantern close to it, studying it with mounting amazement. It had been made by one of her own boots! There was no mistake about it. She was too trail-wise to make a mistake.

But she hadn't been anywhere near Chief's stall tonight.

And the print crisscrossed the mark of the sheriff's heavy boot That meant it had been made since he put Chief into his stall tonight!

She studied the mark again, and was more bewildered than ever. It was the print of one of her old boots—a pair she hadn't worn for weeks! She knew it by the repair patch on the leather sole.

She was still kneeling there, puzzling over it, when she heard the *clop-clop* of hoofs along the road from town. She hastily blew out the lantern flame as the rider turned into the ranch road Then she waited in the darkness, looking out through the open barn doors.

In the bright moonlight she made out the figure of a girl on a tall horse, turning into the stable yard. Now she had the answer to the whole puzzle. The girl could only be Melinda, because the horse was Chief.

Melinda rode up slowly and dismounted just outside the open doors She seemed weary and moved stiffly as if she had ridden a long way and was not used to it She limped a little as she went up to Chief's head and took the bridle to lead him into the barn.

Annie could see that Chief's coat was flecked with foam. She must have ridden him hard! Annie was suddenly angry. Melinda had better have a good excuse for taking Chief without permission and then riding him half to death.

She waited till Melinda had brought Chief inside the warm barn. Then she stepped out and faced her. "Hello, Melinda!" she said coldly.

"Oh!" Melinda gave a startled gasp. "Oh, hello, Annie!"

Annie just stood staring at her, taking in the borrowed clothing and boots, waiting for Melinda to explain.

"I hope you won't mind," Melinda said hastily. "I had such a headache, I thought if I rode out a short distance into the desert it would get better. I borrowed your riding clothes because I didn't have any. Will you forgive me?" She was talking fast and nervously.

"That part's all right, about the clothes, Melinda," Annie told her gravely. "You're welcome to borrow anything I have. But I wish you hadn't run Chief so hard. Uncle Luke won't like it when he finds Chief all tuckered out tomorrow."

"Oh, please don't tell him I took his horse!" Melinda seemed frightened at the idea. "I—I wanted to try riding astraddle the way you do, and the big horse looked so solid and steady."

Annie hesitated. Melinda seemed so distressed, as she stood wringing her hands and looking appealingly at her, that she softened. "Well, maybe if you dry Chief off and brush him down properly, he'll be rested by morning."

"Then you won't tell on me?" Melinda pleaded.

"I won't bring it up unless Uncle Luke does. That's the most I can promise."

"Oh, thank you, Annie! I—I don't want anyone to know I went for a ride. . . ."

Annie looked stern. She disliked hiding things. She was always frank and aboveboard. She said coldly, "Better tend to Chief before he starts getting a chill."

"Oh, I will! Right away!" Melinda told her hurriedly. And then as she started to lead Chief toward his stall, she stopped again suddenly and looked back toward Annie.

Annie had started out through the doors without another word. Melinda suddenly burst into tears, dropped Chief's bridle, and ran after her friend. "Annie, please! Wait!" she called, and the next moment she had thrown her arms around Annie's neck and was sobbing on her shoulder.

Annie's arm went around the older girl, and she let her cry it out for a couple of minutes.

When Melinda's sobs had died down, Annie asked

quietly, "What's bothering you, Melinda? You can tell me."

"I'm so worried about Blair!" Melinda wailed. "I don't know what to do!"

"Of course you're worried!" Annie soothed her. "It must be terrible not to know what's happened to him!"

Melinda lifted her head from Annie's shoulder and drew back a step or two. For a moment she hesitated, trying to decide whether to confide in Annie or not. Then she made up her mind. "It's a lot worse *knowing!*" she said miserably.

Annie was startled and puzzled. "I don't understand."

"That outlaw in your uncle's jail—that man who held up the stagecoach—the one you caught today—is *my brother Blair!*" Her voice broke and she covered her face with her hands and sobbed again.

Annie caught her breath. That *was* a surprise!

Melinda looked as if she might be going to faint again, so Annie hurried her to the old carriage seat against the wall of the barn. "Sit down here while I throw a blanket over Chief. Then you can tell me all about it."

It was soon told. Annie listened silently but sympathetically. "And then he said he *wasn't* Blair!" Melinda said with a sob at the finish. "He sent me away!"

"It might be he's ashamed of the life he's been leading," Annie suggested, "and doesn't want to drag you into it."

Melinda thought a moment, then shook her head slowly. "He would have been different. Annie, he looked at me as if he'd never seen me before! He *didn't* know me, I'm sure of it!"

Annie had another thought. "You only had a quick look at him earlier. Are you very sure he's Blair? He could be somebody else who happens to look a lot like him."

Melinda said with firm conviction, "I know my own brother, even if I haven't seen him for a year or more." Then she gripped Annie's hand and burst out tearfully, "Oh, Annie! What am I going to do?"

"First, you'd better stay away from the jail. If he's trying to protect you, you've got to let him. If people find out he's your brother, it might make things unpleasant for you in Diablo."

"I know. I've thought a lot about it. I almost didn't try to talk to him, because I was afraid Mrs. Gillis might find out somehow."

Annie nodded soberly. "I suppose she *would* make a row about him being an outlaw. The others on the school board wouldn't blame you for things your brother has done, but she would. And she's chairman."

"If I lose the teaching job, I won't have any way to make a living. I'll have to go somewhere else. But I have no place to go." Melinda seemed crushed.

"You can stay here, and welcome." There was no question in Annie's mind about that.

Melinda shook her head slowly. "I couldn't. Not with people pointing at me."

"I guess I know how you must feel," Annie admitted. "Maybe it would be better not to say anything about who 'Bill Welton' is, except to Uncle Luke—"

"Oh, no, please!" Melinda interrupted in a panic. "I know he'd have to put it in his records, and then it would get out. Please, don't tell him yet! Maybe there's some other way around it."

"Well, I suppose it won't do any harm not to say anything to him for a little while. . . ." Annie felt deeply sorry for her.

"Promise, Annie! Promise you won't tell him!"

Annie hesitated. "I'll make a bargain," she said finally. "I won't say anything about it till I've had a talk with Bill Welton—I mean, your brother Blair." She saw Melinda's eyes light up hopefully. "He might have been forced into helping with that ambush. It would be a good idea to get his side of it, if he'll tell it to me. Then when we go to Uncle Luke, we'll have the whole story to tell him."

"Oh, Annie! Would you try to talk to him tomorrow?" Melinda begged.

"I will if I get the chance," Annie promised.

Tagg was sound asleep when she tiptoed into his room. She was glad of that. Tomorrow morning he would probably have almost forgotten about coming into her room to tell her about the open barn doors. If he did remember, it wouldn't seem very important in daylight. She drew the covers up over his shoulders and kissed the top of his tousled head. Then she tiptoed back to her room.

It was nearly dawn before she felt ready to sleep. Then just as she was dropping off, she sat up wide awake. She slipped out of bed, lit her lamp, and sat down to read over the old newspaper account of the disappearance of Blair Murdock. A thought had struck her suddenly, and it seemed to make sense. Suppose Blair Murdock wasn't trying to shield his sister by keeping silent about who he was? Suppose he had been so badly hurt by those Indians that he didn't remember that he was Blair Murdock? Maybe he believed he *was* an outlaw named Bill Welton!

12   Annie Keeps Her Word

Mrs. Sam Gillis was up earlier than usual that Sunday morning. Her husband was surprised to see her finishing breakfast when he came down to the kitchen. She was dressed in her Sunday silk and even had her hat on.

She could hardly wait to tell him about seeing Annie Oakley ride by late last night. He didn't seem to think much of that, till she pointed out that it looked very suspicious. "What do you figure she's been up to? I bet her uncle don't know she's runnin' loose on Saturday night!"

"Better keep it to yourself, Essie," Sam warned seriously. "She might've been on an errand for the sheriff. You don't want to start talk."

"Huh!" Mrs. Gillis tossed her head.

"You sure it was her?" Sam asked.

"I saw her plain as day! Nobody else wears them tomboy

clothes!" She glared at her husband, then frowned suspiciously. "You tryin' to stand up for that little show-off?"

Mr. Gillis denied it hastily and loudly enough to convince her, and peace settled down for the moment. But he
did a lot of thinking. She had made him curious.

After Mrs. Gillis had departed for church under her lace-
trimmed silk parasol, her husband decided to take a little
walk into town himself. Tex had given him a message for
Deuce and Welton last night. What was it he had said? Oh,
yes—that he would get them out of the jail in plenty of
time, long before the wagon was due. He thought Deuce
would be glad to hear that.

He put on his Sunday suit and sauntered up into town.
He was rather proud of his appearance, and bowed with
dignity to the Chet Alberts as they wheeled past in their
surrey. "Good morning!" he called out. "Nice day!"

But Chet grinned, waved his whip, and called back, "Hi
Sam!" quite casually.

Sam looked darkly after the surrey, and then he smiled
and swaggered up the wooden sidewalk. Chet was another
one who would be surprised when Tex Chantry had things
going his own way in Diablo!

He continued on up the street to the sheriff's office. The

door was standing open and there were two horses tied to the rail. He knew them for the sheriff's and Lofty's.

Instead of stepping inside, he slowed down as he came up toward the doorway. Voices were coming out, angry voices. The sheriff and his deputy sounded as if they were having a disagreement. It might be worth while to hear what it was about.

He stopped clear of the doorway and pretended to dust his boots with his bandanna handkerchief.

"I'm telling you again that Annie was *not* here last night!" That was the sheriff's voice, louder than Gillis had ever heard, and angry, too.

Then he heard Lofty answer, and the deputy's words amazed him. "And I'm telling you she was! She came to that cell window back there to talk to one of that pair. I know it for sure because it woke me up, and I got a good look at her when she rode off!"

"Lofty, you couldn't have seen her. She didn't leave our house after we came back from town! We sat around the kitchen and had tea, the two of us. Then she went to bed."

The man who was listening outside the door frowned. "Luke's lying!" he thought. "The Oakley girl *was* in town late last night, because Essie saw her! Somethin's funny!"

He heard the sheriff's voice again. "We'll settle this now. Come on!" And he heard heavy boots cross the floor.

Now the voices had become indistinct. The lawmen had evidently gone back to question the prisoners. Sam Gillis had to hear the rest of this.

He went in and saw them in front of Deuce's cell. He stopped close to the door. If they heard him come in, he would pretend he hadn't heard the argument.

But no one noticed him. Luke and Lofty both had their backs turned. He could hear quite plainly what they were saying. Deuce Adams was laughing at some question that the sheriff had just asked. Then he said with a sneer, "Maybe I saw her last night, and then again maybe I didn't! I don't owe *you* any answers!"

Luke strode to the next cell. "What about you, Welton? Did my niece come here to talk to you last night?"

Sam Gillis had to strain his ears to hear Welton's quiet reply. "Not that I know of. I didn't see Miss Oakley here."

"There, Lofty!" the elderly sheriff turned abruptly to his deputy. "What do you say now?"

"I say he's lying! I say there's something mighty strange going on here!" Lofty snapped back angrily. "Last night Deuce admitted she was here. And I saw her riding away myself. That's enough for me!"

Sam Gillis slipped hastily out the front door. No one had noticed him. He started straight back to the hotel. "Got to tell Tex about this right off," he told himself. "Luke's tryin' too hard to prove Annie wasn't there, an' Welton's siding with him. I don't like the smell of it! Those two are up to somethin'!"

The services had just ended at the little white church up at the end of the side street.

Friendly little groups were gathering for their weekly get-together with old friends and widely separated neighbors. After a little, each family would collect its offspring, gather Aunt Minnie and old Uncle John, and ride on home in the creaking ranch wagon or the family surrey, to the big Sunday midday dinner.

When dinner was over, the ladies of the house would exchange choice bits of gossip they had gathered, while the menfolk dozed during the long drowsy afternoon or just sat around enjoying their one day of rest from the hard labor of pioneer life.

Mrs. Gillis lost no time circulating her story about seeing the sheriff's niece riding recklessly through the Saturday night streets of Diablo. She did her best to make it sound mysterious and somehow scandalous. And most of the ladies agreed that it was very unladylike behavior, to say the least. Somebody, they said, should tell the sheriff that his niece was setting a bad example for the other young people.

Sarah Jane Alberts was one who didn't think much of Essie's bit of gossip. She cut the woman off rudely, with the frank opinion that Essie seemed to be going out of her way to start talk about Annie. "Sounds to me like you're jealous because she caught those outlaws!" Sarah Jane laughed. "Maybe you ought to take shooting lessons and learn to ride a horse! I can just see you now!"

A lot of people heard her, and Essie knew they were laughing. She flounced away to a new group, who was anxious to hear what she had to say. And now she didn't just hint that Annie had been up to mischief. Instead she came out with a flat statement that she had inside information that there was something wrong going on.

Annie and Tagg had come to town in the buggy with Melinda, but Annie had brought along Target, tied to the rear of the vehicle. She had told Tagg that she had an errand in town and would be along later, so he would have to take her place driving Melinda home in the buggy. He had been flattered to think she thought he was grown-up enough for that, so he had agreed at once. Now she and Melinda were waiting for him to bring the buggy around from the shed.

They were standing on the church steps as they waited, and they had a chance for a few last words together without anyone hearing. Annie had the newspaper clipping in her pocket to show the prisoner, if he still denied that he was Blair Murdock. If he had really forgotten, it might jog his memory. On the other hand, if he was only pretending, in order to shield Melinda, he might admit it when he learned that Annie, too, was protecting his sister.

Melinda was feeling happier this morning. When Annie had reminded her of the newspaper clipping, it had given her new hope for Blair. "If he *did* lose his memory when those awful Indians attacked him," she suggested excitedly, "then anything he's done since then shouldn't be counted! I mean, he wasn't in his right mind—so how can he be to blame?"

"I don't know what the law says about that," Annie said gravely, "but I sure hope it would agree with you."

Now Tagg had the buggy waiting. He pulled up at the church steps with a flourish, trying to look very important and grown-up for the benefit of a small knot of his schoolmates watching from the sidelines. "All abo-o-oard, Miss Murdock!" he called out.

"Good luck now," Melinda said hastily, "and thank you, Annie!" Then she drew her long skirts about her and started down the steps.

"See you later!" Annie called after her. She hoped she would have a chance to talk to Bill Welton without her uncle or Lofty being around. But she had no idea yet how she could manage it. She hurried down the steps and made her way around to the shed where Target was tied.

She noticed that a couple of her neighbors gave her sort of frosty greetings, and some of the ladies seemed to be staring at her curiously. She wondered what was wrong with her clothes, but when she glanced down hastily, she didn't seem to have forgotten anything. Her boots matched, and everything was buttoned that should be buttoned. She decided that perhaps she had imagined they were looking at her differently.

She rode slowly down toward the office, thinking over what she would say to Bill Welton when she got the chance to speak to the prisoner alone.

Melinda had just started to get into the buggy when Mrs. Gillis called over to her, "Miss Murdock! I'd like to talk to you." Melinda thought she looked angry at something, and she went back to her when she beckoned.

"I don't want you to think I'm tryin' to set you against Annie Oakley," Mrs. Gillis began, "but you bein' in the pay of the town of Diablo an' the school board, it's only fittin' you should know that some folks in town don't think it's decent the way that girl carries on."

Melinda looked startled. "Why, Mrs. Gillis! I don't understand!"

"I mean," the stout woman said bluntly, "she's runnin' too wild. She was out till all hours of the night last night. People saw her."

"Last night?" Melinda's voice was faint.

Mrs. Gillis nodded grimly. *"Alone!"*

"I'm sure there must be a mistake. Annie was in bed long before midnight. I *know* it!"

Mrs. Gillis' jaws set like a steel trap snapping shut. "I know what I'm talking about. Happens I'm the one who saw her, high-tailin' it out of town like the devil was hangin' onto her horse's tail!"

"Hey, Miss Murdock!" Tagg called from the buggy seat, "this animal's gettin' hard to handle." He was doing his best, but the horse was eager to get started and was getting restive.

"I'll be right there, Tagg!" Melinda was immensely grateful for the interruption. In another second she might have burst out in defense of Annie, and that would have been the end of her schoolteaching. "I'm sure there's some mistake, Mrs. Gillis," she said hurriedly. "You probably mistook someone else for Annie. But if she had been in Diablo late last night, I know she would have had a very good reason for it."

Then she hurried away before Mrs. Gillis could get angry at her. And as she rode out of town in the buggy with Tagg, she thought sickly, "I should have told her it wasn't Annie she saw. But I couldn't—I couldn't!"

Mrs. Gillis looked after the buggy. "She's mighty sassy herself, that one. She better watch who she talks back to. She as good as called me a liar, an' I don't aim to forget it!"

As Annie rode past the hotel, Sam Gillis was just going inside. He stopped to wave to Annie and call good morning. She answered cheerfully and went on.

Gillis looked after her with a twisted smile. "Miss Sly Boots!" he muttered. "You an' your uncle think you're smart, but you got another think comin' when you try to cross me an' Tex Chantry!"

He found Tex Chantry in the deserted barroom, at his usual table in the corner. Tex was counting last night's winnings. He greeted Sam carelessly.

"Pretty good night," he confided, piling up a stack of gold pieces, and hefting a sack of gold dust that sat beside them. "I'm beginning to be glad I holed in here."

"You may change your mind sudden," Sam said sourly.

Tex dumped the gold pieces into his pocket. "What now?"

"I found out Annie Oakley made a quiet little visit to the jail late last night, to talk to Bill Welton through the cell window."

The cold-faced gambler opened his eyes wide in surprise. "How do you figure it?"

"It looks to me like Welton is aiming to make a private deal with the sheriff!"

"What gives you that idea?" Chantry was tense.

"Sheriff and Welton both claim Annie wasn't there, but Deuce and the deputy say she was. They saw her!" Gillis paused to let that sink in, and then added importantly, "And *I* happen to *know* she was in town real late last night."

"You sure?" Chantry eyed him coldly.

"My wife Essie saw her from the bedroom window, when she rode by fast, along toward mornin'!"

Chantry leaned back in his chair and swung his watch chain around and around while he thought it over. Gillis kept his eyes on him expectantly. When Chantry spoke, he was talking to himself more than to Gillis. "I don't know how much Welton knows about my plans for taking over Diablo, but whatever it is, I can't give him a chance to pass it on to MacTavish. Things are shaping up too well to let a cheap hired gun spoil them for me!"

"How can you stop him?" Gillis whined.

"By getting him out of that jail and back to the hills before he gets another chance to bargain with the sheriff!" Chantry said emphatically. "And we'll take care of it today!"

Luke MacTavish was surprised to see Annie come into the office. He had expected her to go back to the ranch with Tagg and Melinda after church.

Annie thought he looked tired and worried. He didn't smile and make her welcome the way he usually did. Instead, he got up slowly and came around the desk to her.

"Annie," he said gravely, laying his hands on her shoulders and looking down searchingly into her eyes, "I'm going to ask you something. I know you'll tell me the truth."

"Of course, Uncle Luke," she said quietly.

"Did you leave the house again last night, after you said good night to me in the kitchen?"

"Why, yes, I did, Uncle Luke," Annie said promptly. "I hope I didn't wake you up."

Luke frowned. His voice was harsh as he said, "And where did you go?"

"Just to the barn to close the doors. Tagg came into my room to tell me the barn doors were open, so I went downstairs, got the lantern, and went out to close them." That much, she thought unhappily, was true.

"And you didn't ride anywhere?" He studied her face.

"Of course not!" She could answer that without lying. "I came back to the house and went to bed." It was still the truth, but not all of it. She had to leave out about talking to Melinda, or she would be breaking her promise not to tell about Melinda's midnight ride into town.

The sheriff's stern expression faded. "Then it couldn't have been you who talked to Bill Welton at his cell window last night!" he exclaimed triumphantly.

"No, it wasn't!" She was startled. So that was what his questions were leading up to. Someone had seen Melinda last night, dressed in *her* clothes. And she couldn't explain without breaking her promise. She could only stand there.

Uncle Luke was jubilant now. He grinned down at her. "I knew all along it wasn't you! But I had to ask you, so I could tell Lofty he'd made a mistake!" Then he stalked quickly over to the door and bellowed, "Lofty! Come here!" at the top of his lungs.

He turned from the door and grinned boyishly. "He's over at the lunchroom, sulking because I didn't believe him. We'll set him straight right now!"

Annie thought, in a sudden panic, "What am I going to say now without dragging Melinda into it? Oh, why did I ever give her my word not to tell?"

13   Out and Away

Lofty Craig came striding across the street from the lunchroom in answer to the sheriff's hail.

In another moment, Annie knew, Luke would be telling the deputy that he had been mistaken in thinking that it was Annie who had visited the outlaws last night and then fled without waiting to explain why she had come there. Annie had a feeling that Lofty would ask her point-blank if she knew *who* had worn her familiar riding habit on that secret visit. Then she would have to break her word to Melinda and tell.

"Guess I shouldn't have tried to hold it back from Uncle Luke anyhow," she decided unhappily. "Telling half the truth never seems to work out right. You just get in deeper." And then and there she made up her mind that the moment Uncle Luke and Lofty walked in, she would start from the beginning and tell them the whole story.

But before Lofty could get halfway across the street to meet the sheriff at the door of the office, a loud clanging filled the air.

Everybody in Diablo knew the meaning of that sound. It was the fire alarm!

Halfway down the street, in front of the Emporium, Sam Gillis was hammering on the big iron triangle that hung from a post at the edge of the sidewalk. As he swung the short metal bar against the triangle, he yelled excitedly, "Fire! Fire!"

The quiet Sunday street came alive in a hurry, as heads started popping out of windows and doors, and people began hurrying toward the general store.

Annie ran to the doorway and saw that far down at the end of the street, smoke was curling up out of the broken front windows of the old abandoned livery stable. It was getting thicker by the second.

"Hurry along! Get the bucket brigade started!" Sheriff MacTavish called to Lofty. "I'll be right with you!"

Then, as Lofty ran down the street toward the livery stable shouting, "Volunteers! Bring your buckets!" the sheriff turned quickly to Annie.

"Look out for things here, Annie. If the fire shows signs of getting out of hand, I'll be back to move the prisoners!" He grabbed his hat and ran out.

Her knees felt weak as she called out after him, "All right, Uncle Luke!" She had to sit down on the step. "That's what Uncle Luke would call 'being saved by the bell,' I guess," she thought, a little dazed.

Now, before she told Uncle Luke about Melinda and her brother, she would have a chance to talk to the outlaw herself. She might even be able to persuade him to turn against his outlaw friends!

She saw that flames were beginning to dart out of the old stable windows, but the bucket brigade was already running with its water buckets to put out the fire. It might not last very long. She had better hurry with her questioning.

She went inside and directly to the cell door. "I want to talk to you," she said sternly.

The tall young man rose from his seat on the cot and came over to the door. As usual, he had a teasing twinkle in his eyes when he looked down at her. "Good morning, . Miss Oakley. Do you need a couple more willing fire fighters out there?"

"Please don't try to be funny, Blair Murdock. This is right important."

"Blair Murdock? That's a nice sounding name," he admitted, "but it isn't mine, young lady."

In the next cell, Deuce Adams moved closer to his door so he wouldn't miss anything.

"Your sister Melinda says that it is!" Annie snapped. "Even if you made believe you didn't know her when she came here last night to see you!"

"So that's who the young lady was! You must tell her I'm sorry she was scared away, but she was wasting her time anyhow. You have the wrong man. My name is Welton, and I am from Texas." He still wore the faint smile.

Annie was annoyed by that teasing smile. "Your name is Blair Murdock and you know it!"

"But I don't!" he laughed.

Annie studied him soberly a moment, and then she noticed the scar on the side of his head above his temple. It wasn't an old scar. It could have been made a couple of months ago. "Where did you get that scar?" she pointed to it suddenly.

Bill Welton looked surprised. His hand went to the scar and touched it gingerly. It still hurt. He smiled wryly.

"That's a sort of very personal question, Miss Oakley," he said, "but I believe it was a gift from the law!"

"You believe it, but you're not sure!" Annie said quickly. "Is that what you mean?"

"He means he got it when he was bein' chased by a posse a couple months ago, Miss Nosey!" Deuce snarled at her from the next cell. "Anything else you wanta know?"

"Plenty!" Annie scowled back at him, and then turned to Bill Welton again. "Don't you remember?"

He looked at her strangely. He was beginning to feel an interest in her questioning. "Not exactly." He touched the scar again. "This—sort of blanked out the details."

"What *do* you recollect?" she persisted eagerly.

"Nothing before Deuce came along and found me crawling on the desert, almost dead, and brought me back to life. But what's all this about?"

Annie thrust the newspaper clipping through the bars. "If you'll read this, maybe you can figure it out for yourself."

At the other end of the street, everyone had been so busy five minutes ago trying to put out the fire, that no one had noticed that Sam Gillis had quietly dropped out of his place in the line of men who were passing buckets of water along from hand to hand to throw on the blaze.

Now he hurried through the deserted alley toward the back of the jail, a heavy six-shooter weighing down his side pocket.

Once there, and after looking around keenly to see that no one was watching, he moved in close under one of the cell windows and listened. He could hear voices in there. One of them was Annie Oakley's and the other was Bill Welton's, but he couldn't hear what they were saying. He moved quickly to the next cell window.

In that cell, he could hear Deuce Adams' voice, only a few feet away, call out, "Don't listen to her, Bill. She and the sheriff are tryin' to befuddle you! They've found out about your gold strike an' they'll try to git it away from you!"

Sam Gillis' eyes narrowed. A gold strike! That was something Tex Chantry would be interested in, if it was worth going after.

Sam reached up to the window ledge and scratched on the stone sill with his fingernail. It made only a tiny noise, but he was sure Deuce would hear it.

Deuce did. He had just started to call out a few more words of warning to Welton, when he heard the faint sound at the window. He suspected what it was, even as he turned his head and stared. He saw the hand. He moved over in two strides and got up on the cot to peer out between the iron bars.

As he looked down, Sam Gillis grinned at him, drew the gun out of his pocket, and handed it up quickly. Deuce grabbed it, and Sam formed two words with his lips, "Horses—alley." He cocked a thumb over his shoulder toward the shed.

Deuce nodded, and Sam moved away rapidly. Deuce watched him hurry out of sight down the alley in the direction of the fire.

Deuce checked the gun hastily. It was fully loaded. Six bullets should be enough to clear their way to freedom. He stepped down quickly from the cot and over to the door, holding the gun behind him so Annie wouldn't see it. He listened.

Bill Welton was speaking. "Some of this seems to fit. It's funny, but Deuce picked up some rich ore that had been dumped near me in the sand. We've always thought I must have made a gold strike out in the hills somewhere before the posse caught sight of me. If it *was* a posse!"

Annie's voice was excited. "It could have been Indians that chased you! That would fit what the paper says!"

"Indians—" Bill Welton seemed to be trying to remember, "sometimes I have nightmares where I can see them coming at me at a gallop, screaming and yelling, waving lances, getting closer all the time . . . horrible, painted faces. . . ." He stopped abruptly.

"That scar on your head could have been made by an arrow just as well as a bullet!" Annie said eagerly.

"I suppose—so—" he said slowly, "but if I'm not Bill Welton, why was I carrying a wanted notice for him in my inside shirt pocket, all folded up tight?"

"Maybe I can answer that!" Deuce spoke up suddenly from his cell. "Lemme show you somethin', Miss Oakley!"

Annie went over unsuspectingly. "What is it?"

Then she saw the weapon in his hand, its deadly nose aimed straight at her heart.

"This!" Deuce Adams bared his teeth in a mean grin.

She saw that the weapon was cocked, and his forefinger was on the trigger. To try to use her own gun would be foolish. She had no doubt Deuce would shoot without hesitation.

"Draw your gun and drop it on the floor right there!" He held the revolver steady on her.

She had no choice. She took her six-shooter out of its

holster and let it fall to the dirt floor.

"Now up with your hands, and kick that gun over here. Pronto!"

Again she had no choice. She kicked it toward the cell door, and it clanged against the iron cross-rail at the bottom. Deuce Adams bent quickly to pick it up, and as he did, Annie half lowered her hands and took a step as if to grab for it herself. But Deuce straightened up hastily with the gun and covered her again. "Oh, no, you don't!" he snarled. "Git back there an' keep those hands up!"

Annie backed off and put up her hands again, but she still watched him closely, hoping to catch him off guard somehow, though it looked hopeless now.

Deuce stuck her .45 into his belt, grinning. "Hey, Bill, I got you a nice gun!" he called. Then he stood close to the cell door, and with his six-shooter only a few inches from the iron lock he pulled the trigger.

The gun roared deafeningly and the cell was filled with flying bits of metal and the acrid smell of gunsmoke.

Deuce kicked the door open and came out, as Annie dropped her hands, wheeled, and started to run for the front door. "Hold it," he barked, and strode after her with his gun pointed, "or I'll shoot!"

She stopped and turned with her hands in the air.

"That's better! And don't try it again!" Deuce sneered. "Now, where's the cell keys?"

Annie nodded toward the nail on the wall where the ring of keys hung, but she made no move to get them.

"Go get 'em and let Bill out! Pronto!" he gestured with his gun.

She went over to them, desperately trying to think of something to do to stop the jail break. Then, as she took the keys down she whirled suddenly, and before he could guess what she was up to she threw the ring and its heavy iron keys straight into his ugly face.

Deuce tried to duck, but the keys hit his forehead and staggered him. He yelped with pain and grabbed his forehead, letting go his gun.

Annie wheeled and ran toward the front door. She had it partly open when something struck her back. Deuce had picked up a chair and thrown it. It didn't hurt, but it knocked her off balance so that she stumbled and fell hard against the edge of the door. She saw a wild burst of stars and flashes of light. Then everything went black and she slumped to the floor.

Deuce strode over and stood with his gun pointing down

at her. For a moment he was tempted to shoot. His forehead was bleeding slightly where the keys had cut it, and it hurt. Then he heard Bill Welton calling, "Hold off, Deuce! You hurt that youngster and every lawman in the Territory'll be hunting you down like a timber wolf!"

Deuce turned, holstering his gun. "Yeah. I guess so. But I ain't aimin' to forget I owe her somethin' for this"—he touched his forehead— "an' I'll pay her off when the time's right!"

"Get me out of here and let's go before somebody comes to see what the shot was!" Welton urged. For the moment he didn't care what his name was or his history. That could wait till later.

Two minutes later the pair were mounted and riding quietly out of Diablo, threading their way through back alleys and cutting off into the hills at the first cross-trail.

The fire was just about out now. Sheriff Luke and Lofty went inside to look around. There wasn't much left of the dusty, rickety old place, but there was a smell of coal oil that made them both sniff suspiciously.

"It was set afire, all right," Luke decided. "But why would anybody do a thing like this?"

Lofty shook his head, puzzled. "It's a good thing Sam Gillis saw the smoke comin' out the window. Most of the town might have gone up."

Sam had come in. His face was smudged from fire fighting. "The town owes you a medal, Sam," Luke told him.

And several other volunteer firemen shook his hand. But Sam got away from them as quickly as he could. He was just a bit afraid one of them might sniff some of the kerosene that he had accidentally spilled on his sleeve when he started the fire!

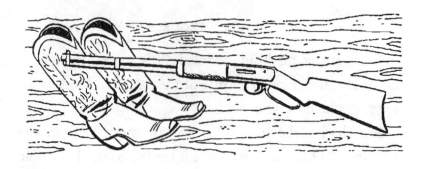

14   Under Suspicion

Annie sat up slowly in the doorway of the sheriff's office. Her head hurt and she had a lump on her forehead where it had hit the edge of the door.

For a moment she was dazed. Then she suddenly recollected all that had happened, and she scrambled hastily to her feet. Both cell doors were standing wide open. The prisoners were gone.

She staggered to the front door and into the street. There was still a crowd around the livery stable, but most of the smoke was gone. Evidently they had put out the fire. She could make out her uncle's tall figure, surrounded by a small group.

She had no idea how long she had lain there unconscious. Not long, probably, but long enough for the escaping men to get well away. She ran around to the back yard. There was no sign of them there. The alley was empty except for a stray dog rooting in a trash can.

By the time she had run back to the street, she saw that the sheriff had detached himself from the crowd and was on his way back to the office with Lofty at his side. She beckoned to him to hurry, and made a sweeping gesture with her hands that told him, in the Indian sign language that they both knew, that there had been a "going away."

Luke caught the meaning at once, and with a hurried word to Lofty, started toward Annie on the run. The deputy followed quickly, and others, sensing trouble, were hard on his heels.

Annie ran out to meet Uncle Luke. "Deuce and Welton broke out and got away!"

"How did they do that?" Luke was astounded.

"Deuce got hold of a gun somehow, held me up, and let Welton out! I tried to stop them, but Deuce knocked me out by throwing a chair. When I came to, they were gone!"

Sam Gillis came panting up and elbowed his way to them. He pointed to Annie's empty holster. "Looks like they got *your* gun!" he said loudly. "How'd they do *that?*"

"Deuce got the drop on me by a trick and made me hand

it over!" Annie told him glumly.

"Tough luck, Annie!" He shook his head sympathetically. "You sure seem to have trouble holdin' onto that young Welton hombre. That's the second time he's given you the slip!"

"What's that got to do with it?" Sheriff Luke glared at Gillis.

"Nothin'. Nothin' a-tall," Gillis assured him hastily. "I was just remarkin', that's all. Didn't mean a thing." Then he added loudly, so nobody could miss it, "Wonder how Deuce got hold of a gun?"

Annie frowned. "Probably got it from the same one who started the fire to draw everybody away from the jail! At least, that's what it looks like to me!"

Luke nodded briskly. "I think the same, Annie. That fire was set, right enough. We could smell the coal oil when we got inside the building."

"Maybe you're right, Sheriff!" Sam Gillis agreed heartily. "The way I see it, somebody slipped the gun to them some time last night. Must have been real late, when nearly everybody was abed. Sneaked around and put it through the cell window, most likely."

Sheriff Luke shook his head gloomily. "Well, how they

did it doesn't matter now. They did it—and those birds are out of the cage and away!"

"I'd sure like to know who it was!" Lofty growled.

Sam Gillis turned to Annie, still keeping his voice at a good pitch. "Maybe *you* saw somebody actin' suspicious when you were ridin' around here late last night. Got any recollection of it?"

"I wasn't riding around late last night," Annie said flatly. "I was at the ranch from eleven o'clock on." She saw a couple of the men look sharply at her, and could feel the tension in the air.

"That's right, she was," Sheriff Luke agreed. "So she can't help us on that!" He turned to Lofty, "Let's go in and see what damage they did!" Then to Annie, "You can tell us just what happened."

But as he and Lofty started into the office, Sam touched her arm and detained her. "I hope you ain't mad at me for tellin' your uncle you were in town late last night. I figgered he knew it."

"He didn't—because I wasn't here," Annie said with a frown.

"That's funny," Sam spoke loudly enough for several listeners to hear him plainly. "Essie was sure she saw you ride by real fast, well after one o'clock! Matter of fact, she was worried your horse would trip an' throw you, goin' so hard!"

"Tell her thanks for worrying, but that wasn't me," Annie smiled. "She needs new glasses!"

She turned and walked toward the office door. But she wasn't smiling. Now she knew why some of the ladies had stared so at her after church. Essie Gillis had been telling them she saw Annie Oakley out late and alone. And now Sam Gillis was making it even worse. He seemed to be trying to hint that it had something to do with the escape of the prisoners.

It was time she told Uncle Luke the whole story about Melinda and her brother. She should have done it at first, she knew now.

She went inside and called to her uncle, back at the cells with Lofty, "Uncle Luke, I want to tell you something."

He came forward at once and stood smiling down rather gravely at her. "I'm ready to hear it, Annie."

"It's about last night. The Gillises are spreading it around that I was here in town very late," she said, "but I wasn't."

Lofty had come up. He frowned. "But, Annie, Deuce Adams told me you came to the window. And I saw you ride away myself!"

"You were wrong, Lofty," the sheriff told him quietly. "Somebody else came here dressed to look like Annie. It's no matter right now who it was. We'll have the final word when we bring in Deuce and Bill Welton and hear what they have to say. Meanwhile, see how many you can round up to ride with us tomorrow and try to find that pair."

Lofty nodded and started for the door. In the doorway he stopped and looked back. "I'm glad it wasn't you, Annie. I couldn't figure it out. But that girl sure looked like you in the dark!" Then he went out, whistling.

Annie said quietly, "I suppose I better tell you who it was."

"You don't need to, honey. I know it was Melinda."

"But how did—" she stammered, "I mean—what—"

"What makes me think so? Well, somebody rode Chief mighty hard last night. And then did a poor job of taking care of him afterwards. I noticed it this morning, but I thought I'd wait and see what came out before I mentioned it to anyone."

"Oh!" Annie waited for him to go on.

"When you told me you hadn't done any riding, I knew it had to be Melinda. Now, let's hear the story."

So she told it, glad to get it off her mind. And when she had finished, the gray-haired sheriff sat silent, thinking it over. At last he looked up and saw her worried frown, and he leaned over and covered her small brown hand with his own and smiled affectionately. "I'm sorry you tried to handle it alone, honey," he told her soberly. "But it's done now. Unless you want to bring Melinda into it, we'll have to let things stand till we get Welton back and I have a talk with him."

Annie nodded slowly. "I guess that's best. People wouldn't believe me if I told the truth now, and it would only make things bad for Melinda. Right away they'd suspect *she* gave her brother that gun."

"That's true," her uncle sighed, "though there are plenty of people right here in town who could have been mixed up in that stage robbery with Adams and Welton. People who didn't want those Texas notices to get to us!"

"Uncle Luke, I think when you catch Bill Welton he'll help you round up the others! He was just about ready to decide he's really Blair Murdock, when Deuce pulled the six-shooter on me!"

"I hope you're right, Annie! And now, all we have to do is find him!" The sheriff frowned and shook his head. "If we can! They could have headed in any direction."

"When he got away from me before, he went straight toward the Black Buttes," Annie said eagerly. "Maybe that's where they've headed."

Her uncle shrugged. "That's a pretty slim lead to go on, hon. Why, we don't even know the color of the horses they were riding, or if they're hiding out in some ranch house or some place right here in town with the friends who helped them get away."

But Annie's hunch was right. The pair were well on their way up to the Halfway House in the Black Buttes.

Starting out in the middle of the day, they had the desert sun to endure all the way across the long sandy stretch of wasteland that lay between Diablo and their goal.

They were both tired out when they reached the lower foothills and felt the fresh breeze off the high snowcaps cooling their faces. They could breathe freely for the first time in several hours, without getting a lungful of dust and sand. Even the horses perked up and wanted to go along at a livelier clip.

As they came onto the higher ground, with huge boulders

and scrub oaks to offer welcome shade, Deuce pulled up
to wait for his tall young partner to catch up with him.
All the way, Welton had stayed a few yards back on the
trail so he wouldn't have to eat Deuce's dust. Now he joined
the older man in the shade of a tall boulder.

Deuce uncorked his water bag and held it out. "Have one
on me, pardner!" he grinned.

His partner drank sparingly and then moistened the end
of his neckerchief and washed some of the sand off his face.
Then he handed back the water bag, smiling. "Very refresh-
ing, thanks. The next one's on me!"

Deuce laughed, but his eyes were searching the younger
man's face with a cold shrewdness. "What do I call you
now?" he asked suddenly. "Bill Welton or Blair Murdock?"

"I've been thinking about that," the young outlaw said
soberly. "I think it's Murdock." He took from his pocket
the newspaper clipping Annie Oakley had given him. "I'm
beginning to remember a lot of things, after reading this
and talking to the Oakley girl. Indians riding at me, yelling
and howling. And arrows whizzing close. And before that,
digging in a hillside and finding a chunk of rich ore. And
riding a long way to Bonanza City to have it assayed." He
stopped, rubbing his hand across his forehead.

"Keep on!" Deuce urged. His eyes were hard, and he licked his lips greedily. "Where was your camp? Where did you dig out the ore?"

"That's what I don't remember!" Blair Murdock shook his head and scowled.

"But you've gotta remember, pardner! That's the thing we been tryin' to find the answer to ever since I found you almost dead on the desert, and saved your life!" He put a heavy underlining on the last four words.

"I know! I'm trying to bring it back, but it won't come!" Murdock covered his eyes with his hand and tried to think. "I can see a tall pine tree—so it must have been higher in the hills than this. There was a hillside, and rocks. I dug every day in the outcrop. I recollect killing a rattler on a ledge outside my diggings. But I don't remember where the diggings were."

"What about a map? You must've drawn a map so you could register your claim!"

"If I did, it was probably in the saddlebags that were dumped out beside me, and the wind blew it away."

Deuce flashed a suspicious look at him, but was reassured by Murdock's blank expression. "Did you file on it when you were in Bonanza City? The clipping says you hired a horse there, so maybe you filed the claim there."

"I'm sure I didn't," Murdock frowned. "There was some reason. Let me think. File. Claim. Assayer. That's it!"

"What's *it?*"

"I didn't file the claim at Bonanza City because I didn't trust that assayer. He asked too many questions about where the ore came from. So I decided to wait till I got to Diablo and file it there. But I never got there. . . ."

Deuce had been holding his breath. Now he let it out with relief. "Well," he grinned, "all we can do is keep tryin' and you'll get the whole thing straight some day soon. Then we'll both be rich!" He looked slyly at Murdock. "I'm still in for a share like you promised, ain't I?"

"Of course you are! You saved my life, whether it was a posse bullet or an Indian arrow that laid me out in the desert! Half of my gold strike is yours, no matter how big it turns out to be!"

"I figgered you'd still feel that way." Deuce grinned and held out his hand. "Shake, pardner!"

"You bet!" Murdock smiled back at him, and shook his hand warmly, without suspecting that Deuce had already made up his mind that once he got the half, he would see to it that the rest would be his without much delay.

15   The Lost Trail

Early the next morning Sheriff Luke and his deputy left the office at the head of a small group of determined men.

It was going to be difficult to pick up any trace of the fugitives, because so many people had come to Diablo on Sunday, for the weekly church services and to visit with friends on the one day of rest, that nobody seemed to be able to remember two ordinary-looking men riding out of town.

But Sheriff Luke and his posse divided up into twos and threes, and fanned out in all directions from the center of town. All day long they rode in ever-widening circles through the surrounding desert, stopping at each remote ranch house or lonely line shack to question the people there. But no one remembered seeing two men ride by, one very tall and the other short and squat.

Along toward evening the posse began its weary return empty-handed, to meet at the sheriff's office.

As Sheriff Luke and Lofty rode past the hotel, tired and dust-covered, Sam Gillis and Tex Chantry watched them from the cool shade of the hotel porch.

Sam Gillis put down the tall glass of lemonade that he was sipping, and leaned out over the porch railing to call to the lawmen. "Any sign of 'em?"

Luke MacTavish shook his head and rode on.

Tex Chantry swung his watch chain and yawned. Then he spoke lazily to Sam Gillis. "I've been thinking. That gold strike you heard Deuce speak to Welton about might be worth looking into. Suppose you go fishing again tomorrow and see what you can find out about it up at Halfway."

Sam Gillis looked pained. He dreaded making that long, hot trip again. Besides, he was afraid to try to sneak out of the house again so soon. Essie was still talking about the last time, morning, noon, and night. "Maybe they didn't go straight up there. Might be better to wait a coupla days."

Chantry smiled coldly. "Suit yourself. If you can't arrange to go tomorrow morning, I can find somebody else who'll be glad to do it for me. Maybe that would be better in the long run anyhow."

Sam's face turned pale. "Oh, no! I'll do it, Tex, if you say so. Very first thing in the morning."

Tex Chantry's smile was warmer now. "Good! The sooner we find out whether it's worth going after, the better."

Sam agreed hastily. He felt better, hearing Chantry say "we." For a moment there, he had felt left out in the cold. And he didn't want to risk that, no matter how much Essie yapped.

At the schoolhouse, Melinda was finishing up her first long day of teaching. The pupils had had to be sorted out and seated in the big classroom according to the grade they were supposed to be in. The eighteen of them were all ages and sizes, and it was puzzling to her, a stranger.

Most of the children had seemed to enjoy her confusion, but Tagg Oakley had been a big help. He had found the former teacher's papers for her, tucked away in a drawer of her desk, and with those records to help, the rest had been simple.

It turned out to be not half as bad a day as she had feared, once she had gotten used to the sound of her own voice giving orders, explaining problems, and impressing certain rebels with the fact that she would stand for no misbehavior.

Now, as she prepared to close up the schoolhouse and drive back to the ranch, she heard someone ride up. Her heart gave a jump. Maybe it was Blair! She had a sudden wild hope that he had come back to try to straighten things out, now that he knew who he was.

But it wasn't her brother. It was Annie. And from her excited expression as she ran toward the doorway, she was bringing news. Melinda hurried to meet her.

"Did they find Blair?" Melinda demanded. "Does he remember who he is?"

Annie faced her with a smile, but shook her head. "No, they didn't find him, but—"

"Oh!" Disappointment darkened Melinda's pretty face.

"—but I just talked to Uncle Luke and told him you were wondering if the law would excuse your brother for the things he did when he thought he was a wanted outlaw." She paused, her eyes sparkling. "And he says it might be so!"

"How wonderful!" Melinda exclaimed.

"And tonight he's going to ask Dr. Busby about it, when he drops by the ranch for supper. Doc knows a lot about the fine points of law."

Melinda's brow wrinkled. "I hope Dr. Busby won't let anyone know Blair's my brother! It would be sure to get back to Mrs. Gillis!"

"Uncle Luke and I wouldn't tell Doc if we didn't know he could be trusted," Annie reminded her soberly.

"Mrs. Gillis would be sure to think I gave Blair the gun he used in his escape!" Melinda wasn't convinced yet.

"Right now, from the way Mr. Gillis talked yesterday, she thinks *I* did it. And we're going to let her think so, if she wants to, till Uncle Luke can straighten things out for your brother. All she can do is guess and gossip. And words can't hurt me when I know they aren't true."

"Annie, I'll never forget all you're doing for me," Melinda told her. And a few moments later they went to the buggy with their arms around each other's waists, and were cheerful all the way home, Melinda driving and Annie riding alongside on Target.

Blair Murdock, away up in the Black Buttes, had few reasons to be cheerful, though he was freed and safe from the approaching Tumbleweed Wagon of the law.

For one thing, ever since Deuce Adams had found out that instead of being Bill Welton, hunted outlaw, his tall young partner had been an honest prospector with no criminal record, he had changed.

Instead of being willing to wait till Blair could remember where he had made his gold strike, now Deuce kept hammering away constantly at him. "Think, man! Take a look at it!" He held a chunk of the rich ore up to Blair. "Remember where you dug it out!"

And when Blair tried hard to bring back the memory, and drew a blank, Deuce turned on him angrily and accused him of holding back and trying to keep the gold strike wholly for himself.

Stung by the accusation, Blair Murdock denied it angrily and flung the ore aside before he stalked across the room to sit in front of the fireplace, head in hands.

It was Cookie who tried to make peace between the partners. He liked Blair Murdock, no matter who he was. "Now, looka here, Deuce," he argued, "you'll just get the young feller more mixed up than ever, fussin' at him! Let him be! He told you half the strike was yours, an' it's my guess he'll stick to that."

"He'd better!" Deuce muttered, glaring across the big room at Blair.

"Knew a feller like him once," Cookie went on, "clear

lost his memory. Couldn't call back even his name, till they took him home to the old farm an' he ran into his gran'ma. She figgered he was funnin', an' she fetched him a clip on the ear with her wooden mixin' spoon, like she used to do when he was a young-un. An' by jinks, it brought him out of it faster'n greased lightnin'!"

Deuce grunted and waved him away. "Stop yappin', an' rustle up some supper."

It was a silent meal. At the end of it, Blair Murdock rose suddenly and walked toward the door. He stopped to take his gun belt from its customary nail, and began to buckle it on. Before he could finish, Deuce had moved swiftly and stood in the doorway barring his way.

"Where d'ya think you're going?" he asked abruptly, his eyes hard and suspicious.

"Anywhere," Blair answered shortly, "just so it's away from here. I don't like being accused of being a liar."

Deuce could see that he meant it. And there was nothing the outlaw could do to stop him. Murdock's revolver (it was Annie Oakley's loaded Colt .45) was in his gun belt, but Deuce's gun was twenty feet away, hanging on a nail.

Deuce grinned sheepishly at Blair Murdock. "Aw, you know I didn't mean what I said! I was just tryin' to help you remember. Thought maybe if I riled you up a little, it might jolt you into it."

But Blair Murdock, looking down soberly into Deuce's grinning face, saw the cold, unsmiling eyes and knew that Deuce was no longer his friend. It was a shock to the younger man to see the mask of friendliness slip off, revealing the evil of the man who had called himself his partner for the last few months.

Murdock knew suddenly that he was in danger. The gold lust had been in back of all Deuce's show of friendship. If he tried to leave now, it was almost certain that he wouldn't get far before he would be caught and brought back, this time as a captive. He would have to wait his chance to get away.

He decided he would play along with Deuce, pretending to believe him. If some day he did remember where he had dug that rich ore, he would keep his promise and divide fairly with the outlaw who had saved his life.

So he hung up his gun belt again and made Deuce think that he believed what he said. They sat down with Cookie and laughed over the memory of Annie Oakley's angry face when Deuce had surprised her with the gun Sam Gillis had brought him.

"Sure got the drop on Miss Sharpshooter that time!"

Deuce laughed. Then, touching the cut on his forehead that she had made with the bunch of keys, he added viciously, "Too bad you got chickenhearted, Bill. You shouldn't have stopped me when I had a chance to finish her off. I got a feelin' we'll have trouble with her again!"

"Not me!" Blair Murdock laughed. "I've seen my last of Diablo and that lady tornado!" But at the same time he was thinking that he would try to see his sister Melinda some day soon, even if only to let her know that he was safe, and would do nothing more to disgrace her.

Down at the sheriff's Bull's-Eye Ranch, the big lamp on the center table sent a soft yellow glow on the faces of the four people who sat around it and talked far into the night.

Outside, tied to the porch, Doc Busby's old buggy stood waiting, with Miss Lightnin' patiently leaning into her harness and resting her ancient bones. She had grown used to waiting for old Doc in the past decade, waiting sometimes all night while he sat at the bedside of the sick and dying.

"There might be a chance the law would hold that your brother wasn't himself while he was breakin' the law," Doc told Melinda gravely, "but he'd have to show the judge an' jury that he'd lived a different kind of life since he found out who he was!"

"I'm sure he will!" Melinda told the others firmly.

"If he gave himself up," Annie asked thoughtfully, "would it count in his favor?"

"I should think so," Sheriff Luke agreed. "What say, Clem?"

Busby nodded. "Trouble is, he probably wouldn't know that!"

"If we could only get word to him!" Melinda's hands were clasped tightly as she looked into their kind faces. But no one seemed to have an answer for that. The posse had searched pretty thoroughly without success.

Then a voice came from the stairway. It was Tagg, who was supposed to have gone to sleep hours ago. "I bet Annie and me could find him! Couldn't we, Annie?"

"Scoot right back to bed, young feller!" Annie called out sternly. "The only finding you're going to do, is finding your way to school tomorrow morning! And see that you're down to breakfast on time or Melinda'll drive off without you!"

"But, Annie—" he started. Then he saw Annie start to get up from the table, and he ran upstairs. When they heard his door close, Annie and her uncle and Doc all laughed, but Melinda only sighed and continued to look miserable.

A few minutes later, as Sheriff Luke stood beside Doc's buggy and said good night to him, Doc looked a little worried. "Now, you lay down the law to that Annie child. I saw a gleam in her eye I didn't like, when that little rascal talked about finding Murdock. First thing you know, she'll want to try, and she'll most likely find herself in the middle of a hornet's nest. There are more outlaws than those two runnin' loose up in our hills!"

"I'll keep an eye on her!" Sheriff Luke promised sternly.

And when he went inside, he told Annie that she wasn't to try to find Blair Murdock. "It's up to him now," he reminded her and Melinda. "If he deserts his outlaw friends and comes in to give himself up, it'll be in his favor. If he has to be hunted down and brought in, that's different!"

So Annie gave up a half-formed plan to try to pick up Blair Murdock's trail, out where he had given her the slip after the stagecoach robbery. That was a little-used trail, and she had felt sure she could pick up some sort of a track to follow there. But now all she could do for Melinda was try to comfort her with cheerful words, while they waited for Blair to come in and surrender—if he ever did.

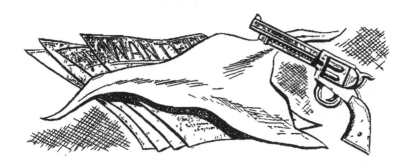

16 · A Surprise or Two

Annie lay awake a long time that night. In spite of what she had told her uncle about not minding Mrs. Gillis' catty gossip about her, it bothered her a lot that she couldn't straighten it out. But that would have meant involving Melinda, and she couldn't do it.

Then there were Mr. Gillis' hints that she hadn't tried very hard to stop the outlaws from escaping, and might even have helped them. She didn't know if he really believed such nonsense, but he certainly had seemed to be trying to give people that impression.

It was hard to understand why Sam Gillis would turn on her. He had been very friendly all along. As a member of the town council, he had been Sheriff Luke's strongest backer in the fight to keep the town free of the riffraff that was overrunning it.

"Maybe he's tired of being nagged by Essie all the time, and he just has a 'down' on all the women," she decided sleepily. "I think I'll go and talk to him tomorrow morning."

And she went to sleep at last, feeling that it should be easy to convince Sam Gillis that he had made a mistake.

When she woke up in the morning, it still seemed a good idea, and she was cheerful and relaxed as she saw Melinda and Tagg on their way to school in the hired buggy.

She was tempted to tell Uncle Luke what she had decided to do, but at the last moment she changed her mind. He had enough on his mind, without her adding to it something she could easily straighten out herself.

Annie ran after her uncle as he was riding away, and called to him, "I'll see you in town this morning, Uncle Luke. I have some things to tend to and some shopping to do."

"I don't figure on being around till late today, honey," he told her. "Lofty and I are going out alone to look for those two in a couple of places we couldn't cover yesterday. There's an abandoned mine up on Sawtooth Peak we may look into. It's a likely place to hide."

"Be careful, Uncle Luke!" she called after him. "They're

a tricky pair!" And she waved to him.

He waved back at her with a smile and rode away.

It was a couple of hours later that she tied Target to the hotel hitch rail and went inside to look for Sam Gillis.

The lobby was deserted except for Jake, the night clerk, tipped back in his chair behind the desk, sound asleep.

She went up to the desk and waited. He looked so comfortable that she decided not to wake him. She started to go out, intending to come back later when Mr. Gillis himself would probably be on duty.

But as she turned to leave, Tex Chantry, the gambler, came down the stairs from his room and strode up to the desk. It was the first time Annie had seen him close up, and her nose wrinkled disdainfully at the smell of lilac water that wafted her way. He was certainly what Doc Busby would call a "fancy gent," with his diamond stickpin and the flashing ring on his right hand.

He rapped loudly with his key, and when the dazed Jake stumbled to his feet and came to the counter with a hasty "Good morning, Mr. Chantry," the gambler ignored the greeting and turned to Annie instead.

"Good morning, Miss Oakley," he said, with a tug at his

elegant small mustache. "We haven't met before, but I'm Hamilton Chantry, and I've admired your skill with the rifle and revolver for a long time."

"Why, thank you, Mr. Chantry!" Annie said cordially.

"I hear that some of the good citizens of Diablo are thinking of electing you sheriff in place of your uncle this fall!" He sounded almost serious, but the smile he added to the words was sarcastic and Annie's face flushed with anger.

"If that's supposed to be a joke, Mr. Chantry," she said angrily, "I don't think much of it!"

"A joke? I hardly think so. You seem to do better at catching lawbreakers than your uncle does—even if you do let them go again!" And he laughed.

Annie turned her shoulder to him and spoke abruptly to Jake. "I'd like to speak to Mr. Gillis, please."

Before Jake could speak, the gambler answered lightly, "If you do, you'll have to yell real loud, Miss Oakley. I hear he's gone fishing up at Lost Lake!" And he strolled over toward the barroom door without waiting for a reply.

Annie glared after him, her cheeks flushed and burning. Tex Chantry was one of the principal men her uncle wanted to run out of Diablo. There had been complaints that he was a crooked dealer, vague reports of men whom he had "skinned." But none of the victims had wanted to make a formal complaint against him, though the sheriff had tried to urge them to it. They had all backed away at the last minute, and Sheriff MacTavish had come to the conclusion that for some reason they were afraid of Chantry.

Jake saw her angry expression, and leaned over the counter to whisper, "Don't mind him, Miss Oakley. He's a smart aleck that just likes to stir folks up."

But Annie was thinking now of something Chantry had just said. She asked, frowning, "Did he say Mr. Gillis had gone fishing up at Lost Lake?"

Jake nodded and looked sour. "Yeah. I dunno why he went there again. He tried it a coupla days ago an' came back empty-handed. Didn't even get a bite."

Annie looked thoughtful. There was something funny here. If Gillis said he was fishing in Lost Lake, he told a lie. Because Lost Lake had been dried up since the middle of April! The big ranchers north of there had dammed up the stream that fed the lake, to flood their grazing lands. She and Tagg had discovered that just a few days ago, on one of their "explorations."

"Today was my day off," Jake was complaining, "but he went just the same. It ain't fair, Miss Annie. He didn't even let me know he was goin' till last night. I'm gettin' sick of it."

"I don't blame you, Jake!" Annie agreed heartily. Then she said quietly, "Well, when he gets back I wish you'd tell him I'd like very much to talk to him about something."

"Oh, he'll be back real early," Jake grinned, with a wicked glint in his eye, "seeing he forgot to take his pole an' line!" He cocked his thumb toward a pole which was standing in the corner behind the desk. "I saw him leavin' it, but I was so mad I just let him go without it. Wow! Will he be sore when he gets to the lake an' finds out he has no pole!" He chuckled with satisfaction.

But Annie frowned. She was thinking that wherever the hotel man had gone, it hadn't been to catch fish. Not in Lost Lake, anyhow. And that was the only place within twenty miles where there ever had been enough water this time of year to promise a mess of fish!

Jake, having started complaining, kept on. "The boss ain't the same man he used to be, Miss Oakley. He's been took in by that Chantry feller, with his talk about making Diablo a big town and such like. It's given Sam ideas!"

"What sort of ideas?" Annie encouraged him. Maybe she was getting on the track of something!

Jake looked around quickly to see that no one was in the lobby but themselves. Then he took a small mirror from the drawer. "Wait till I show you this!" he grinned.

He held the mirror so that it reflected some blotted signatures on the desk pad. They were backward, but the mirror turned them right side to, and Annie could read them quite plainly.

"I just happened to notice these today. It's Sam's writing," Jake said eagerly.

Annie read the signatures, all written with elegant flourishes. "Samuel Gillis, Sheriff of Diablo County" was one of them. Another was "Sheriff Sam Gillis," and as Jake moved the mirror over another couple of inches she read, in the boldest writing of all, "Sheriff Samuel Quincy Gillis."

"Well!" She smiled up at Jake. "It looks like I'm going to have some opposition when I run for sheriff like Mr. Chantry says!" And she laughed lightly.

But a few minutes later she was quite thoughtful as she led Target up the street toward the sheriff's office. She decided to wait around in town a little while, in case Uncle Luke and Lofty got back early from their search for the outlaws.

She felt pretty sure that her uncle had no idea that his fellow council member had set his sights on the sheriff's job. Or that, according to Jake, Tex Chantry was behind it.

That might account for Sam Gillis' trying to start talk against her. He probably thought it would reflect on the sheriff!

The trail guard, Tim Johnson, was almost dozing at his post up near the Halfway House, when he heard Sam Gillis' horse plodding up the trail.

Johnson had had a rough night, with almost no sleep. That Deuce Adams and his partner had been arguing and gabbing in the big room till almost daylight, and they hadn't bothered to keep their voices down. He had yelled to them a couple of times, demanding quiet, but that had only made Cookie wake up and get sore at him. He'd had to cover his head with the blanket finally, before he could get any rest.

He sprawled out against a sun-warmed boulder, his rifle close at hand. From his lookout above the trail he could see the faint cloud of dust that told him someone was coming up. In a moment he recognized Sam Gillis.

He stuck his head over the edge of the lookout rock as

the hotel man rode up. "Hi!" he called good-naturedly, "You came back here in a hurry, bud. You must like travelin' the desert!"

Sam Gillis was hot and tired and in no mood for chatter. He glanced up sourly and didn't bother to answer. He turned his horse to start up the twisting little arroyo that led to the house.

Tim Johnson's eyes hardened. Thought he was too good to pass the time of day, did he? He lifted the rifle and aimed at a rock a few feet ahead of Gillis' horse and over to one side. He pulled the trigger, and the gun roared.

Lead smashed against the rock and spattered in all directions. The horse squealed with fright, bucked, and almost threw the hotel man. He hung on, yelling, his arms tight around the horse's neck. For a moment, it looked as if he would go heels over head into the cactus.

Up above, Tim Johnson grinned happily as he ejected the empty cartridge case and put in a new one. He watched the struggle of man and horse with keen interest, and was a bit disappointed to see Gillis manage to stay in the saddle and regain control of the excited horse.

When Gillis had the horse calmed, he glared up at the guard. "What was the idea of that?" he yelled.

Johnson leaned over the edge of the boulder. "Rattler! He was coiled an' ready to strike!"

"I don't see any rattler!" Gillis glared around at the rocks and brush.

"I musta missed the durn thing!" Johnson said cheerfully. "Anyhow, I skeered him off! An' you're welcome to the favor!"

"Well, thanks," Gillis growled, and rode on up the arroyo, grumbling to himself as he went.

The guard grinned broadly after him, and leaned back against his rocky perch. Maybe next time, he thought, Gillis would stop to say hello.

The shot down on the trail had put the men at the house on guard, but a few minutes later the *caw-caw* of a crow signaled them that the approaching person was friendly.

All three were surprised to see Sam Gillis. Deuce and his partner were glad to see him, so they could thank him for helping them break out of the jail. But Cookie wasn't so friendly. He promptly took his rifle and departed to hunt for some wild game. Somebody else could rustle up a free meal for stingy Gillis!

It didn't take Sam Gillis long to notice the strain between Deuce Adams and his young partner. He took the first chance he could get to ask Deuce what was wrong.

"Nothin'," Deuce answered shortly. He had no intention of telling Gillis about the gold strike.

"What's eatin' Bill?" the hotel man persisted. "Look at him!"

The young man was staring gloomily out the narrow window across the room from them.

"Bill? Oh, you mean Mr. Blair Murdock! That's his right name. He ain't Bill Welton any more!" Deuce sneered.

"Murdock?" For a moment Gillis puzzled over the name. Then he remembered where he had heard it before. "Why—that's the new schoolteacher's name. He must be—"

"The missing brother!" Deuce finished it for him. Then he explained hastily how Murdock had lost his memory and then regained it. "It was the sister that came to talk to him the other night, not Annie Oakley," Deuce explained, "but it wasn't till yesterday, when the Oakley girl showed him a newspaper clippin', that he started rememberin'."

"Does he remember all about his gold strike?" Gillis inquired eagerly. "Is it a real good one?"

"What gold strike you talkin' about?" Deuce asked.

"The one you're afraid the sheriff is after! I heard what you said about it, when I was at the cell window!"

"Oh, *that!*" Deuce looked at him out of the corner of his eye. "I was just jokin'. There's no gold strike."

Gillis' face fell. "That's sure too bad! Tex Chantry was figgerin' to let you boys buy in on his big deal in Diablo. He'll be sorry to count you out!"

"Wait a minute!" Deuce had changed his mind suddenly. "What's the deal?"

"He's bringin' in a string of gambling houses and casinos, and building a first-class hotel. All he needs is twenty thousand or so."

Deuce cast a quick look toward the tall silent man across the room, and his voice was carefully guarded as he spoke. "Bill's got a gold strike, sure enough. From the looks of the ore he dug out of it, it's worth ten times a measly twenty thousand! Only—he claims he can't recollect where the ore came from!"

"Can't or won't?" Gillis asked shrewdly, keeping his eye on Blair Murdock and his voice low.

"I haven't figgered that out yet. He claims he's tryin'."

"If he's telling the truth, he won't mind lettin' us help him. Get him over so I can talk to him!"

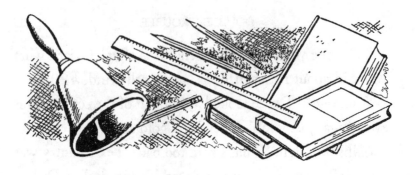

17   A Strange Sort of Map

Blair Murdock seemed willing enough to talk to Sam Gillis about his "lost" gold strike, but he still stuck to his story that he had no idea where it was. He guessed that it might be somewhere in the desert hills between Bonanza City and Diablo, but that was a lot of ground to cover, and it still could be in some other direction.

Sam Gillis was inclined to think Murdock was telling the truth, but Deuce was still sullen and suspicious. "What about a map? Stands to reason you must've drawn one if you had any idea of staking and registering the claim!" Gillis persisted.

"We thought of that right away," Murdock told him, "but the only paper Deuce found on me was this Wanted notice, folded up small in my inside coat pocket." Murdock handed a well-worn printed sheet to Sam Gillis.

Gillis carefully smoothed it out on the table and stared disappointedly at it. "William Welton, bank robbery, stagecoach holdup, train robbery. Hmmm! The description sounds a mite like you, though."

"That's why I figgered he was Welton, or he wouldn't have had it hid so careful," Deuce explained. "Too bad I was all wrong."

But Sam Gillis, smoothing the paper with his hand as he read it through, had felt something. He quickly turned the notice over and felt the other side. Then he held it up so that the light from the window was behind it. He studied it closely and then exclaimed, "Hey! This looks like some sorta map! It has words and lines punched in it!"

Deuce snatched it and held it up in front of his own eyes. The light came through in a thousand pinpricks that seemed to be arranged in a pattern. "Here's what we've been lookin' for, Bill!" He grinned happily at Murdock. "Take a look and see if it means anything to you!" He was his old self again, friendly and warm.

Murdock looked through the pinpricks and nodded slowly. "It's certainly a map. Here's the word 'pinetree,' and a cross below it. That could be where I dug out the ore." He studied it again. "It says 'dry wash' below here, and here's 'road to Diablo' along this wavy double line!"

"Great!" Deuce was grinning from ear to ear.

Murdock dropped the paper to the table and shook his head grimly. "But there's nothing to show where on the road to Diablo those landmarks are!"

The two men stared at him in dismay. Deuce's face darkened with anger. "You *know* where they are!"

"I wish I did!" Blair said quickly and earnestly. "The way I feel about this whole thing now, I'd tell you in a flash, and get out of these buttes as fast as I could travel! I don't want any part of it!"

The other two exchanged uneasy looks. He sounded as if he were telling the truth.

Then Deuce spoke suddenly. "I got an idea! I heard the Oakley gal tell you in the jail that your sister read her a letter you wrote about your claim. Maybe you told her *where* it was, in that letter!"

"I'm sure I didn't!" Murdock could see where the question was leading. "She doesn't know the country, and the names of any places I might have written down would have meant nothing to her."

"Still, it's worth lookin' into," Gillis said, nodding to the impatient Deuce.

"That's just what we'll do!" Deuce assured him. "It'll be easy to find out, if she kept your letters."

"I won't have my sister dragged into this!" Murdock exclaimed angrily.

"You got no choice, Murdock," Deuce said coldly. The friendliness had gone again. "It's out of your hands."

"But I know it's bound to come back to me soon where the spot is," Murdock argued. "Just give me time. Keep away from my sister. I've caused her enough grief already."

But they drew away from him and refused to make any promises. A little later when he happened to glance at his gun belt hanging on its nail, Murdock saw that the .45 they had captured from Annie Oakley was no longer in his holster. And neither Deuce nor Sam Gillis would admit that they had taken it. Since the guard, Tim Johnson, had been around and in and out in the last few minutes, and was now headed back to his camp at the lookout point, it seemed possible that he had taken it.

Murdock decided to say no more about it, but to go secretly to Cookie, when the little fellow returned from his hunting trip, and borrow another gun.

Once he was armed, he would watch for a chance to slip away. He had no idea where he would go. But wherever it was, he would begin a new life. And if he had good luck, he would make a home for Melinda and himself somewhere where he wasn't branded an outlaw.

An hour later, when Cookie came in with the haunch of a newly killed buck slung over his shoulder, he found Deuce and Sam standing over Blair Murdock and telling him what to write in the note he was sending to his sister in Diablo.

Cookie could see that Murdock was writing it against his will and under threat of the six-shooter that Deuce carelessly twirled over his forefinger close to Murdock's head.

When the note was finished and addressed, Deuce snatched it up, read it over, and thrust it at Sam Gillis. "You know how to get it to her," he said grimly. "Better start down pronto."

"You're wasting your time," Blair Murdock scowled at them as he rose and stalked away.

"You oughta be glad we are willin' to do it," Deuce told him meaningly. His mouth widened in an evil grin. "It gives you a couple more days to jog your memory. If we don't get the answer from the letters, we'll have to find a way to help you remember. An' I don't figger you'll like that!"

Cookie, listening, winced. He knew Deuce Adams was a cruel man, from the way he treated his horse. He felt sure Deuce would go to any lengths to get the secret of the rich ore from Murdock. For a moment he was almost inclined to take a hand and help Murdock get away. His rifle was in reach, and Deuce and Gillis were off guard.

Then he sighed and shook his head, and put the rifle in its rack. After all, he enjoyed his easy life up here at Halfway House, and he couldn't take sides and risk losing it! He began to skin the deer.

Annie Oakley rode toward home at her uncle's side. He was weary after a long, fruitless search for the fugitive outlaws. She hadn't told him about her discovery of Sam Gillis' ambitions, because he seemed tired and discouraged.

He spoke after a long silence. "Funny thing! When Lofty and I were coming down the side of Sawtooth Peak a while ago, we spotted Sam Gillis riding this way across the desert from the north. He was moving right along like he was in a hurry to get home for supper."

"From the north? The Black Buttes?" Annie asked quickly.

Her uncle smiled. "I hardly think so. There are too many

outlaws up that way to interfere with his fishing."

"Fishing? Huh!" Annie exploded. "His fishing's only a fake, Uncle Luke." And she told him about Sam Gillis' pretended fishing trip to a lake that she and Tagg knew had been dry for months.

"Well, honey," the big sheriff grinned at her, "I guess if I was married to a nagger like Essie Gillis, I'd head off·by myself whenever I could, no matter what fibs I had to make up to get away!"

"Well, I bet he's up to something!" Annie insisted stubbornly. "Let me tell you what Jake showed me!" And she told him about Gillis' "sheriff" signatures on the blotter.

This time Sheriff Luke laughed right out at her serious expression. "Why, Annie! That's nothin' to get het up about, child! Anybody can run for sheriff. Maybe the town needs a new sheriff, at that. And you can't blame Sam for being ambitious!" He sobered a moment later. "Though there are others I think would do better in the job than Sam."

"Jake says Tex Chantry, the gambler, gave Mr. Gillis the idea," she said, frowning.

"Maybe so—but I doubt it. It's more likely Sam's sick of working for nothing in his wife's hotel." He leaned over and patted her shoulder as they rode side by side. "Outside of Jake's gossip, youngster, what have you got against poor Sam?"

"Just a feeling, I guess," Annie answered thoughtfully, "and the way he tried to start people thinking I let those two men get away!"

Melinda met them at the door of the ranch house. She was worried. The ladies of the school board had called on her at school and had been very friendly. They had seen the story in Mr. Wiggins' *Gazette* today about Blair being lost on the desert and a prey to renegade Indians. They had come to offer sympathy and reassure her that she would be offered the teaching position for all next year.

"They were so kind," she almost wept, "even Mrs. Gillis! I know I should have told them Blair is alive. But I couldn't! I knew what it would lead to!"

"Don't worry about it," Annie reassured her, "because by the time next school term gets here, everything will be straightened out for you. I'm sure of it!"

"I hope so!" Melinda dabbed her eyes with her dainty lace handkerchief and added mournfully, "Oh, I wonder why Blair doesn't come back to see me!"

"He will, I'm sure! Maybe it isn't so easy for him to get away from his outlaw friends right off, but I bet he'll do it soon!"

It wasn't till after the second recess next day that Melinda received her brother's note. When she rang the hand-bell to call the pupils in for their last hour of study and recitation, Tagg hurried to her desk with the folded note.

"This was stuck in the pump handle, Miss Melinda! Somebody must've put it there since lunch time!"

She looked startled as she saw her name on the outside of the note in her brother's familiar handwriting.

"I heard somebody ride by while we were singin'," Tagg volunteered. "Guess he left it, whoever he was."

She stared at the folded note. She knew that every eye in the classroom must be fixed on her. She wanted to open the note at once, but she didn't dare. She smiled instead, and nodded to Tagg, "Thank you, Tagg. You may take your seat now." When he had turned away, she quietly slipped the unread note into her handbag and began to question the four fifth graders about geography.

But it was hard to keep her mind on what she was doing. She tried, but with half an hour still to go before dismissal time, she rose suddenly from her chair, holding her hand to her forehead, and announced to the amazed and delighted pupils, "School is dismissed. Please file out quietly and go straight to your homes. I'll see you all at nine in the morning."

They succeeded in getting out of the door quietly enough, but once outside they scattered hastily and with wild yells disappeared in no time at all. The older ones hurried because they didn't want to be around in case Miss Murdock suddenly remembered that she hadn't assigned them any homework, and the young ones were just plain happy to get an extra half hour in which to romp.

But Tagg couldn't hustle off. He had to share Melinda's buggy ride back to the ranch. "A lot of good it does me to get off early," he muttered crossly as he hitched the hired horse to the buggy.

But when he had finished doing it, there was no sign of Melinda. So he tied the reins to the hitching post and went to sit under his favorite tree in the back yard. He had to stay within earshot, because she would be coming out at any moment, he expected, ready to leave.

Inside the schoolhouse Melinda opened the folded note with trembling fingers. "My dear sister Melinda," it began.

What a strange way for Blair to address her! He *always* started with "Dear Linny."

"If you have kept any of my letters," the note read, "please get them and bring them with you, after sundown, to the fork in the Diablo road where the Soapstone Trail starts. I will meet you. Do not mention this to anyone. Blair."

She had all the letters Blair had written her since he left home. She had saved them so that when they were settled again, in a new home, they could read them over together and laugh or feel thrilled at the adventures he had had in the West. They were all in her carpetbag at the ranch.

It was almost three o'clock now, by the wooden Seth Thomas clock on the wall behind her desk. Sundown was at six thirty. She would have just enough time to get to the ranch and pick up the letters, and then drive to meet Blair. It was nearly three miles from the ranch to the fork in the road where the Soapstone Trail started.

She excitedly tossed the letter aside, as she rose to her feet and reached for her long shawl draped across the back of her chair. She ran down the aisle and out the front door to the waiting buggy. Hastily untying the reins, and without giving a thought to Tagg, she climbed in, picked up the reins, gave the horse a quick cut with the whip, and drove off at top speed.

Under his tree, Tagg was carefully balancing a reluctant red ant on the end of a long green blade of grass, when he heard the buggy wheels roll and the horse's heels clip-clop.

He jumped up and stared after the fast-moving buggy, too astonished to yell. When it turned a corner and disappeared in the direction of the ranch, he stood a moment pulling at his ear. "Huh! She forgot me! I guess I walk home!"

But first, there was the front door of the schoolhouse standing wide open. Queer that Miss Murdock should rush out and leave it unlocked! He decided he had better get the extra key out of her desk drawer, and lock up before he started his two-mile walk home.

He didn't notice the crumpled note on her desk at first, but as he started away with the key he saw it. "Wonder if I oughta read it," he poked at it with his finger.

But Annie always said it was wrong to read other people's mail unless they invited you to. So he sighed and put it into his pocket. He would take it home and give it to Melinda. She probably forgot it and would be glad to get it again!

He went out, carefully locking the door behind him, and sauntered on home, taking time to do all the important things along the way, like chasing stray butterflies and whistling at a kangaroo rat that hopped away, chittering indignantly at him.

He was in no hurry to get home, and by the time he arrived there he had almost forgotten he had Melinda's mysterious note in his pocket.

18   Trail Into Trouble

Tagg was just turning into the ranch yard when Annie came riding from the barn on Target. She made a fast dismount at his side. "Where on earth have you been? Why didn't you come home with Melinda?"

Tagg grinned broadly. " 'Cause she rode off and forgot me!" Then he frowned, puzzled. "Didn't she tell you?"

Annie shook her head and looked worried. "No, she didn't say anything at all to me. I was ironing in the kitchen, and she just ran upstairs and ran out again a couple of minutes later. I knew it was earlier than usual for you two to get home, and I thought it was odd she didn't stop to say hello!"

"Golly, maybe her headache got so bad she didn't feel like talking," Tagg suggested.

"Her headache? Is that why she came home so soon?"

Tagg nodded solemnly. "I guess so. She put the note in her bag, and then pretty soon she got a headache and let us out."

"What note?" Annie asked sharply.

"Oh, I forgot you didn't know about it. Here it is. She left it behind, so I brought it home for her."

Annie glanced at the crumpled note in her hand and saw the last words, "Do not mention this to anyone. Blair."

"Are you gonna read it?" Tagg asked eagerly.

"I think I'd better. It's from her brother!" She glanced hurriedly through it. "She's gone to meet him!"

"Maybe he's goin' to give himself up and come in!"

"I'm afraid not! He says here not to mention it to anybody. That sounds more like he's decided to stay on the owl-hoot trail!" She shook her head sadly. "Poor Melinda!"

"I bet he'd change his mind if *you* talked to him!" Tagg had a lot of confidence in his big sister.

"It's worth trying!" Annie made up her mind in a flash. "Target can move faster than that old horse and buggy!" She swung into the saddle. "I'll try to get to the fork before he's gone again!"

She pulled her rifle out of the saddle holster where she had thrust it a few minutes ago before starting out to look for Tagg. It was loaded and ready to use. If Blair Murdock refused to see that it would be better for both Melinda and him to give himself up, she might be able to persuade him at least to come in and let Uncle Luke talk to him at the ranch. Once she had the drop on him, he would have to listen to reason.

Tagg stared after the fast-disappearing horse and rider, and pouted. At least Annie could have invited him to ride along. Pixie could keep up with Target, he felt sure, if he coaxed her enough.

Then he grinned as he thought of something. Annie hadn't asked him to come along, of course, but she hadn't said he mustn't! He ran to the barn as fast as his legs would carry him, and in less than five minutes he came riding out as fast as he could make Pixie travel, and set out after Annie.

When Annie was still some distance from the place where the old Soapstone Trail branched off the main road, she could see the buggy. It was empty. The horse was grazing peacefully in the shade of a clump of cottonwoods beside the road, but Melinda was gone.

When she was a few yards away, Annie swung from the

saddle, dropped the reins over Target's head, took her rifle from the saddle holster, and went on foot toward the empty buggy.

Melinda's Paisley shawl lay half in and half out of the buggy, the end of it dragging on the ground. Annie felt alarm as she saw that.

She bent quickly to search the ground, and found what she had been looking for: Melinda's dainty footprint, mingled with that of a man's high-heeled riding boot.

The sand had been kicked up here, close to the buggy. Melinda's heel marks were deep, as if she had braced herself and tried to hold back against someone stronger than herself. Then, as Annie tracked them away from the buggy, Melinda's prints just disappeared, and the unknown man's retreating footprints were pressed deeper into the sand as they led away toward the cottonwoods.

Annie read the answer clearly. The man, whoever he was, had pulled her away from the buggy against her will, and had finally had to pick her up and carry her to where the trampled ground showed that his horse had waited.

The hoofprints leading away were also deeper in the sand than the ones left by the rider's horse as he approached the cottonwood clump. That could only mean that the

horse had carried away a double load, the rider and Melinda.

Annie had had only one talk with Blair Murdock, but she felt sure he wasn't the kind to have dragged his sister roughly from the buggy and ridden off with her, leaving her shawl trampled in the dirt.

It was likely that she had met Deuce Adams instead of her brother! And the whole situation seemed to indicate that the two Murdocks were in trouble.

"I'd better get to Uncle Luke at the office," she thought, running back to Target. But as she started to swing into the saddle, she suddenly remembered that her uncle and Lofty had planned to ride to Smoke Tree Station and try to meet the Tumbleweed Wagon that was due there today. There would be no one at the office. If she wanted to do anything to help Melinda, she would have to do it alone. And she had better start right now, while there was still daylight.

She was heading Target toward the cottonwood grove, to follow the clear trail of hoofprints, when she heard someone riding rapidly from the direction of the ranch.

It turned out to be Tagg, riding as fast as she had ever seen Pixie move.

"Hey! Wait for me!" he yelled, and, "Where's Miss Melinda?"

Annie stopped and waited for him to come up. "She's gone with whoever it was that met her."

"Wasn't it Mr. Murdock?" Tagg looked puzzled.

Instead of answering Yes or No, Annie pointed to the boot prints, "There are his tracks. See what they tell *you!*"

Tagg leaned over and studied them eagerly. Then he straightened up, shaking his head. "It wasn't Mr. Murdock. He's a heap taller than this man. If he had feet this small, he'd sure tip right over if he tried to walk!"

"Good scoutin', young'un!" Annie agreed. "We'll make a real trailer out of you yet! Dad would be proud of you!"

Tagg grinned happily, but there was a wary look in his eye. "Then can I go with you?"

Annie looked grave. "I was going to ask you to take the buggy to town and wait for Uncle Luke. You can tell him where I've gone."

Tagg's face got long. "But, Annie. How can *I* tell him, when you don't know, yourself?"

Annie's eyes crinkled at the corners. "You know, Tagg Oakley, that's a very good question! Maybe we'll send old Red here back to the ranch by himself. And you can help me trail Melinda. But soon as we find out where she's been taken to, I'm sending you back, pronto!"

"That's fine, Sis!" Tagg was happy. "I'll go straight off, soon as you say so!"

Annie hurriedly tied the buggy reins to the whipsocket and started the old hired horse back toward the ranch. He went willingly enough, and Annie was sure that he wouldn't loiter along the way. He knew there would be a good supper of oats waiting for him in the ranch barn.

The late afternoon sun had dipped almost to the horizon. It would soon be gone, and then there would be only the long spring twilight in which to follow the tracks of the heavily loaded horse.

The Soapstone Trail was little used now. A wider, more direct road to the new mining town high in the hills had taken its place, once the rich gold veins had been discovered. Freight wagons filled with furniture or foodstuffs, mining equipment and clothing, and all the things that suddenly wealthy men felt they needed and would pay well for, had to go by the shortest route. So the new road had been blasted out, through the rock-strewn wastelands, and the old winding trail abandoned.

Annie was grateful for that. The only tracks besides

those left by the horse she was trailing were old ones, almost all of them filled with drifting sand and dead foliage. It was easy to keep on, as long as the twilight lasted.

The trail went on among huge rocks and tumbled boulders, winding and twisting as it had since the Indians had made it long ago, as a path to the higher hills.

Then, turning a rocky corner, she and Tagg came upon the spot at the foot of a hill where tall Blair Murdock had escaped from her and left her without a horse. And there in the distance, crossing the wide desert valley, was the trail up into the Black Buttes that he had taken with the two horses. Far along it, silhouetted against the last red brilliance of the sunset, moved a lone horse.

It was too far away to make out who was riding it, but Annie was sure that there were two figures in the saddle.

"I see them!" Tagg exclaimed. "Come on! We can catch up if we ride hard!"

"Uh-uh!" Annie shook her hear soberly. "If it's the one I think it is on that horse with Melinda, we might ride into a shower of lead! We'll take it a little easy, now we know which way they're heading. They can't go very fast riding double, and when they stop to rest we can sneak up on them."

So they rode along at an easy pace on the desert trail. It climbed slowly into the first foothills, and from time to time they caught a glimpse of the horse and its riders.

The twilight was still lingering when Annie heard hoofbeats coming along behind her. She turned in the saddle for a hasty look, but the great chunks of rock that strewed the landscape kept her from seeing back more than a hundred yards or so.

"Somebody's coming behind us! Cut over behind those big rocks!" she told Tagg hastily, and they both wheeled and rode off the trail to disappear behind a clump of granite boulders.

They had only a minute or so to wait before two riders came into sight, riding at a lively clip.

"Maybe it's Uncle Luke and Lofty!" Tagg whispered.

But Annie shook her head. "They went south to Smoke Tree today. No such luck!"

When the two riders were almost abreast of the rocks, Annie leaned over and put her hand over Target's nostrils to keep him from whinnying at the passing horses and revealing that she and Tagg were there. Tagg quickly followed suit with Pixie, but as the two men rode by, the little pony tried to pull its head free, and, failing that, snorted and stamped the ground.

Annie stiffened, her hand going to the rifle in her saddle holster. She strained her ears to hear if the two riders changed pace or showed any signs of having heard the pony. But they continued on their way at the same lively trot.

She sighed with relief and relaxed. "Phew!" she let out her breath gustily. "I thought for a minute that spoiled animal of yours had given us away. But I guess they were making too much noise themselves to hear Pixie."

"Who were they, Sis? Did you know them?"

"I did," Annie answered sternly. "One was Mr. Samuel Quincy Gillis. And the other was that big-talking gambler feller, Chantry."

"Golly! What are they doin' ridin' away up here?"

"I guess Uncle Luke won't take long to figure that out when we tell him!" Annie's pretty face looked grim. "He won't think Jake was just gossiping now!"

"D'you suppose they're headed for the same place as the other man an' Miss Melinda?"

"Hard to tell, hon," Annie replied gravely, "but I hope not. That would sure enough change the odds against us, and they're not good as they are!"

Tex Chantry and Sam Gillis had ridden on less than a quarter of a mile, when Tex suddenly pulled up and announced brusquely, "We'll wait here a bit!"

The twilight was starting to darken, and Sam Gillis was beginning to dread the prospect of that last climb up into the buttes. It was bad enough in the daylight.

"Why?" he whined. "It ain't far to the house now. That's tricky going up there. We could fall a couple hundred feet if our nags made a misstep in the dark!"

"It'll be moonlight in half an hour!" Chantry told him impatiently. "Stop sniveling. We're waiting to see who was staked out behind those rocks back there, watching us go by." And he led the hotel man a few yards off the trail into tall underbrush.

"I don't see nobody coming!" Sam Gillis was scared. He searched the darkening road. "You sure?"

Chantry nodded grimly and motioned Gillis to keep quiet. In the stillness, they began to hear a faint sound of hoofbeats that grew steadily louder. "This time," Chantry had an evil glint in his eye, "we'll do the spying!"

A few moments later he suppressed an angry exclamation as he recognized Annie Oakley and her brother. "So that's who it was!"

Sam Gillis was panicky. "If they were watchin', they must have recognized me! That means I'm cooked so far as Diablo goes!" he whispered hoarsely.

"Maybe not!" Tex Chantry unlimbered a long-nosed pistol.

"Hey! Wait! Don't get her started shootin' at us!" Sam warned hastily.

Tex Chantry began to take careful aim at the taller figure as the Oakleys came abreast of their hiding place. "Leave it to me!"

But in spite of the growing darkness, trail-wise Annie had seen where two horses had turned abruptly into the brush, and she suspected an ambush. She reached over suddenly and grabbed Tagg's arm. "Jump!" she ordered. "And run quick! Get behind those rocks!"

Tagg obeyed without question. He jumped down and scrambled for the shelter of the rocks. The moment he was out of the saddle and running, Annie grabbed her rifle out of the holster, threw herself off Target's back, and ran after her brother.

Across the trail in the thicket a pistol exploded, and a bullet whined past and flattened itself on a rock ahead of her. She jumped the last few feet to safety behind the rocks with Tagg before the sniper could draw another bead on her.

Once she and Tagg were out of the line of fire, Annie readied her rifle and waited for the sound of a movement from the other side of the trail.

The wind was up now, as night started to close in, and it had the chill of high snow-peaks in it. She hoped they wouldn't have to wait too long here in its blast.

"Did you get her?" Gillis asked anxiously. Something was making him shiver. It wasn't only the cold wind.

"Not yet!" Chantry snarled. "But the minute she tries to get to those horses, I'll have her!"

"I don't like this!" Gillis whined. "Maybe we're bitin' off more'n we can chew!" He huddled on the ground behind the brush.

"Shut up!" Chantry glared at him. Then as he looked back across the trail toward the rocks, something moving caught his eye. It looked like a hat of some sort, caught by the wind. Chantry kept his eyes fixed on it, his gun poised. For a second or two the hat rolled aimlessly, a toy of the breeze. Then a stronger gust caught it and flung it back a few feet toward the rocks, to drop it only a long arm's length away.

A small arm reached out quickly for it, but was withdrawn again at once when it owner found he couldn't touch it.

Chantry's eyes glittered icily as he trained his pistol on the edge of the rock.

Then, as the wind moved the hat a few inches still farther out of reach, Tagg leaned out from behind his rock and made a grab. This time he caught the hat by its brim and drew it toward him.

Annie had seen him lean out, and she reached hurriedly for his other arm, to yank him in out of range But before she could haul him to safety, the man on the other side of the trail tightened his finger on the gun trigger, and a shot -blasted across.

He stood staring through the smoke as he heard the boy's shrill cry of pain, and a smile of satisfaction grew on his hard features.

Gillis, crouched beside him, looked up shivering. "Which one?" he asked through chattering teeth.

"The kid!" Chantry holstered his pistol. "She'll be too busy taking care of him now, to do any more spying! Come on, let's be on our way!"

19   The Outlaws Make Plans

But they were not quite through with Annie Oakley yet!

She saw with one swift glance that the bullet which had struck Tagg in the forearm had made only a flesh wound, painful though it would be.

She jumped up and aimed her rifle after the two men who were riding swiftly away. She pulled the trigger, and Sam Gillis gave a yelp of terror as he felt his hat suddenly yanked off his head to spin through the air and fall ahead of him in the dirt.

Chantry heard the shot and put spurs to his horse. He galloped ahead without waiting to find out what had happened to his companion, but Gillis was close behind him. The hotel man was too terrified to know if he was alive or dead right then. He only wanted to get out of Annie Oakley's range!

In less than a minute, even the echoes of their hoofbeats had died away.

Annie was shaking with anger as she bandaged Tagg's arm. "It's only a deep scratch, button," she assured him tenderly. "We'll let them go—for now—and start right back home."

But once Tagg was sure that he wasn't going to die at any moment, he began to feel as good as new. Flesh wound or not, he had been wounded in the enforcement of the law, in a sort of a way. And it made him feel very grown-up all of a sudden.

"I want to get you to Dr. Busby right away and get this dressed properly," Annie told him.

"You don't have to worry about me!" he assured her. "Why can't we keep on just the same? You still don't know where they've taken Melinda."

She stared angrily in the direction Tex Chantry and Gillis had gone. "I bet that's just where those two are headed, too!"

"Let's find out! I feel fine!" Tagg stood up and stuck his chin out bravely. The wound hurt a lot, but he was determined Annie wouldn't have to give up the search for Melinda on his account.

"Are you dead sure, hon?" Annie asked solemnly.

"Cross my heart," he answered promptly. "It hardly hurts at all, except when I move it!"

"Well, we'll try then," Annie decided, "but if it's too much for you, we're going back, Melinda or no Melinda!"

"I'll let you know, honest!" the boy assured her.

But before they mounted again, Annie ran up the road and picked up the hat she had shot off Gillis' head. It was a hat like thousands of others, flat-topped felt with a wide brim and a plain leather band. But there were three initials neatly embroidered in the lining, probably by Essie. They were "S.Q.G."

Annie crushed the hat and rolled it as small as she could, and shoved it into her saddlebag. It was a piece of evidence that might very well send Mr. Samuel Quincy Gillis to the Territorial Prison for a term of years for attempted murder!

It was almost dark now, but a bright silver moon was peeking over the edge of the desert hills and beginning to flood the trail with its pale light.

The Oakleys rode on more slowly now. But up ahead, the two men were moving along at a fast clip. Sam Gillis kept looking back and muttering unhappily to himself. He had

had big plans for his future. Now they were destroyed. And there was nothing he could do about it, except to tag along with Tex Chantry.

Chantry rode ahead, ignoring him. The gambler had no remorse because he had shot the Oakley boy. He wished heartily that it had been Annie, the constant stumbling block in the path of his ambition.

He had heard Gillis' report on the stubborn refusal of young Murdock to reveal where he had found the very rich ore. And he intended to put an end to Murdock's rebellion. He was pretty sure that, between them, he and Deuce Adams could find a way to change Blair Murdock's mind and force him not only to tell them, but also to lead them to his gold strike.

It didn't worry Tex Chantry that Annie Oakley had recognized him. He didn't care whether or not she hurried back to the sheriff of Diablo to tell her story. Once the gold strike was located, he wouldn't need to go to Diablo again. What would happen to his tool, Sam Gillis, didn't worry him in the least. Sam had ceased to be useful.

Up at Halfway House, Deuce Adams rode into the clearing with Melinda on his saddle in front of him. Cookie came out, holding up a lantern, as Deuce pulled in his horse.

"Give me a hand here!" Deuce called, and when Cookie ran over, Deuce lifted the half-fainting Melinda down. She staggered and would have fallen if Cookie hadn't caught her by the arm.

"Who's this?" Cookie demanded angrily. "I thought you went to pick up Murdock's letters!"

"I got 'em! But his li'l sister here pulled my mask off, so I had to bring her along to keep her from rushin' to the sheriff!" He grinned. "She's goin' to be what the Injuns call a hostage. We keep her here till Murdock makes up his mind to give us some information."

"I don't like it!" Cookie growled.

"Nobody asked you," snarled Deuce. "Get her inside and let her talk to Murdock. I got a hunch he'll start gettin' his memory back pronto, when he sees her here!"

Cookie glowered after him as Deuce led his horse to the corral. Then he gently helped Melinda as she stumbled along at his side toward the house.

"I'm sorry, ma'am," he told her in a hurried whisper, "but if you *could* get Bill—I mean, Murdock—to tell the boys what they want to know, it'd be better."

But Melinda was too frightened and exhausted to do

more than let out a tearful sob as he led her to the open doorway.

She stopped there, staring around the lamp-lit room for her brother. Then she saw him sitting uncomfortably straight on a bench close to the fireplace. She called out, "Blair!" and hurried toward him, holding out her arms.

But Blair Murdock couldn't put out his arms to catch her, or even get up to meet her. He was securely roped to the bench, his hands tied behind him. He could only stare at her in horrified surprise.

She sank to the dirt floor beside him, clinging to him and sobbing.

Deuce stalked in with his saddlebags over his shoulder. He called over to Murdock, with a mocking pretense of good humor, "Thought you'd like a visitor. Tell him to be a good boy, ma'am, an' do like we tell him from here on in!"

The squat outlaw sat down at the pine table and dumped a score of letters out of the saddlebags. He opened the first one and started to read it.

Cookie disappeared for a few moments, and then came back with a bucket of fresh drinking water. He filled a tin cup and took it to Melinda. "Drink this, ma'am," he advised, "it's nice an' cool." And then after a hasty glance over his shoulder toward the busy Deuce, he whispered to Blair, "Better give in an' tell him about that gold strike, in case it ain't in the letters."

"I would if I could," Blair replied in a whisper.

Cookie went back to stewing the venison for supper, shaking his head and muttering uneasily to himself.

Deuce had read only a few of the letters when Tex Chantry and Sam Gillis arrived.

Melinda, huddled against her brother near the fireplace, was horrified to recognize the town councilman here in the outlaw camp. And Sam Gillis, in turn, seemed shocked at sight of her. He avoided meeting her eyes, and seemed to have something on his mind that worried him.

But Chantry greeted her with mocking politeness and welcomed her to their midst in flowery language. Then he sat down with Deuce and grimly skimmed through the letters, one by one.

When he threw the last letter aside, he turned and stared across the room at Blair Murdock. "Sort of close-mouthed about it, even to her, weren't you? Too bad!" He turned back to whisper something to Deuce Adams that startled the outlaw for a moment, and then twisted his face into an evil grin as he nodded agreement to Chantry.

A few minutes later, when Tim Johnson came in off guard duty for the night, the two whispered their plan to him and were pleased to see his shocked expression. "Well, I dunno—" he shook his head and gulped as if the thought of what they intended to do worried him. "Maybe it'll work," he finally said grudgingly, "but—suppose he don't remember in time?"

"He will!" Tex Chantry said confidently.

From time to time, during the rest of the evening, Tim Johnson stared at the pair and shook his head grimly. But, though Cookie tried to coax the information out of him slyly, he wouldn't let slip what Chantry and Deuce had told him about their plans for Blair Murdock.

And Sam Gillis, for once in his life without appetite even for the tasty venison Cookie served for supper, was silent and morose and vanished early to bed. He couldn't get the thought of Tagg Oakley out of his mind.

In spite of the moonlight, Annie found the steep trail up into the rugged buttes a difficult one. She kept an eye on Tagg from time to time, and slowed her pace so it wouldn't be too hard on the wounded youngster.

After a more than usually hard climb, she rested Target at a wide spot in the trail and turned to speak to Tagg who was coming close behind her. She was just in time to swing out of her saddle and get to his side before he toppled over into her arms.

She lowered him gently to the ground and knelt beside him. His face was drawn and white, even in the moonlight, but he opened his eyes and tried to smile as he whispered, "Sorry, Sis. I just got kinda dizzy. I'll be okay when I rest a minute."

"Sure you will!" Annie laid her hand on his forehead and found that he was feverish. She was angry with herself now for letting him try to come up here with her. And now that they had ridden so far, there was no chance of getting him back to the ranch tonight.

She stood up and looked around in quiet desperation. In the distance a coyote yipped mournfully, and nearer at hand a mocking bird gave out a lovely trill from the top of a stunted pine tree. But Annie was too worried to enjoy his efforts.

"I'm—c-cold!" Tagg's teeth chattered as the wind swept across the rocky trail.

Annie thought, "I've got to find some sort of shelter!"

and she stared into the deep blue shadows of the hillside, hoping to see a spot that seemed out of the wind, where they could spend the night. But the rocks were all scattered, and not one of them promised to furnish a refuge.

Annie hurriedly took off her leather vest and draped it over Tagg's shoulders. He was too tired and sick even to protest.

When she stood up again for another look around, she was just in time to see Pixie disappearing around the corner of the hill, along a narrow ledge that she thought must have been an animal trail. "I'll be right back, hon!" she said softly to Tagg. "Don't move. And just keep covered."

Then she set out after the straying pony, thinking crossly, "We're not in enough trouble, but Pixie has to add another load!"

But as soon as she had turned the corner on the narrow pathway, she forgave the pony, and even had a hug for him when she caught up with him. For, there, only a dozen feet beyond the turn, was a shallow cave, just exactly the right size to hold one pony, one horse, one hurt boy, and one very thankful girl. And there was dry firewood piled high inside the cave, and a little cache of dried prunes, jerked venison, a can of tomatoes, and some matches. The

venison was ancient and beyond use, thanks to the gnaw-
ing of some woods animal, but everything else was usable.

She started a small fire inside the mouth of the cave, and
saw by its light that a rusted pickax and small spade still
leaned against the rear wall in a pile of rubble. There was
an ancient Navaho blanket, well chewed in places, but
still promising some warmth from its wool. She took it to
the cave mouth, to shake the ancient dust out of it, and any
spiders as well. Then she spread it carefully near the fire
and went to bring in Tagg, and, once she had him settled,
Pixie and Target as well.

It took her quite a while to get them all taken care of,
and then she sat for a long time, staring out at the moonlight, thinking about the situation. Along toward morning
she went to Tagg and felt his forehead.

To her great relief, his fever was gone. He was sleeping
comfortably. She went back to the front of the cave and
lay down with her rifle close at hand, and her head pillowed
on her arm. In a few moments she was sound asleep.

There was no sleep at all that night for Sheriff Luke
MacTavish.

He had ridden into Diablo long after dark with Deputy

Lofty. They had had their long trip to Smoke Tree Station in vain. The Tumbleweed Wagon had not arrived there yet, and Jim Castle, the superintendent, had had no word when it would come. So the sheriff had returned to Diablo without the information he had hoped to get from the United States marshal who was in charge of the wagon on its sweep across the Territory.

He and Lofty had decided not to stay on at the station, though Jim Castle had invited them cordially. There was enough mischief going on in Diablo when the riffraff knew he was on the job, and it might be much worse if he stayed away another night and day.

So they had ridden the long miles back to Diablo, tired and disappointed.

Things seemed quiet enough when they arrived there, except that Essie Gillis came hurrying out of the hotel lobby to stop them and demand that they go looking for Sam. He had left without a word early in the morning, and hadn't come back.

The tired sheriff told her, "If he isn't back by morning, Essie, I'll send somebody out to try to find him. But he's probably just fishin' as usual, and he'll be back any minute."

She had a pointed comment to make on his lack of help

when honest people like her needed his services, and then flounced off angrily.

Luke looked after her and sighed. "Wouldn't blame him if he forgot to come back. That jawin' must get real tiresome!"

"A man's better off without any ties!" Lofty stated.

"Depends on the ties, Lofty!" the gray-haired sheriff smiled. "Now *me,* I don't know what I'd do without mine!"

A little later, as he rode into his ranch yard, he found the house dark. That was unusual because Annie always kept a lamp lit in the living room to welcome him at night.

Then he found the hired horse and buggy standing out in the yard. And in the barn, two empty stalls where Target and Pixie should have been!

He ran to the house, but there was no sign of either Annie or Tagg, and Melinda's room was empty, too.

He waited during the long hours of the night, hoping they would come straggling in.

Then, as dawn streaked the sky, he saddled up his tired horse again and set out for Diablo without a backward look at the empty house. He knew that if anything had happened to those young'uns, he would never live there again.

20   Conflicts

The early morning sun was warm at the mouth of the man-made cave in the hillside when Annie awoke and looked at her strange surroundings in sleepy surprise. Then, in a flash, she remembered all that had happened and sat up quickly.

She felt worried when she saw that Tagg was not asleep on the old blanket where she had left him last night, but she got over it quickly when she saw him sitting outside in the sunshine, grinning in at her.

"How does your arm feel?" she asked quickly.

"Just a little stiff. It doesn't hurt a bit now," he answered cheerfully. "I'm sure hungry, though."

"How about some prunes and stewed tomatoes?"

Tagg's face fell. "Is that all we have?"

"We're lucky to have that much, thanks to some old

prospector that went off and forgot them!" Annie assured him, as she started to count out the prunes, share and share alike.

So they breakfasted on canned tomatoes and prunes, and the food didn't taste half as bad as Tagg thought it would. "But," he said glumly, "I hope we don't have that for dinner, too!"

"We'll be home by then, button," she smiled.

But Tagg was feeling too well now to want to turn back. "Why can't we go on and see if we can find Melinda? We can turn back early, if we don't pick up her trail. Please?"

"Are you sure you feel all right?" she asked soberly. "Let's have no more being brave and strong this morning."

"Honest, Sis!" He stood up and showed how he could move the wounded arm without wincing. "See? Let's go, huh?"

In a few minutes they were back on the trail again, and moving up once more. They tried to make as little noise as possible. Annie had tied strips of the old hole-y blanket to both Target's and Pixie's hoofs, so they wouldn't strike sharply on any stones and advertise that they were climbing up the trail.

The trail was well-traveled, judging by all the hoofprints

on it, leading both up and down. Annie looked back often
to see that no one was behind them.

It was an hour or so later that she pulled Target in suddenly and signaled a stop to Tagg. She had smelled smoke,
not of a cooking fire, but the rank-smelling sharpness
of an old pipe.

They both sat quietly, and in a few seconds they heard a
loud yawn from up the trail somewhere. There was no
sound of anyone coming down the trail, so Annie guessed
that the yawn had come from somebody who was stationed
to watch the trail for intruders.

She slipped out of her saddle and pulled the rifle out of
her scabbard. Then she led Target back to Tagg and handed
him the reins. "Take both of them behind those scrub pines
over there," she whispered, "and try to keep them real
quiet. I'm going to look around up ahead, and see if we can
get by without gettin' caught!" ·

When Tagg and the animals were safely off the trail and
partially concealed among the pine trees, Annie went
stealthily up the trail, careful not to start even a small rock
rolling. After a few yards the smoke smell became stronger,
and then she saw a thin little spiral of it curling up from the
flat top of a tall boulder beside the trail.

The crown of a wide-brimmed hat showed for a moment as the man on top of the boulder moved about. His perch was shaded from the hot sun by a tall pine tree growing up beside the boulder. "A nice cozy spot for a lookout," she thought, "and practically on top of the trail!"

She heard him knock out his pipe on the rock and then yawn loudly and grunt a couple of times as if he were settling down to take it easy. She held her rifle poised, in case he poked his head over the edge and looked down the trail toward her. But a moment later she was relieved to see the soles of his boots stick out over the edge. He was evidently lying down now, taking it easy.

The top of his boulder was a good ten or twelve feet above her. She couldn't get the drop on him without climbing up there. And he might not be as sleepy as she hoped. If she tried challenging him from below, all he had to do was keep down out of range.

She had to find some other way of getting Tagg and herself past him. No use trying to slip by. The clink of a bridle or a snort from the unpredictable pony would alert him. And after what happened last night, she knew that these outlaws wouldn't stop at anything.

She had just about decided to turn back and return to

Diablo. Uncle Luke could hunt for Melinda with his posse. But the posse might get here too late to help Melinda and her brother! She couldn't give up now.

Then she noticed something hanging from the tree limb that shaded the drowsy lookout's post. It was a hornets' nest. If that should drop onto Mr. Lookout, he would be very, very busy. Much too busy, she hoped, to guard the trail.

But how could she jar the nest loose without firing a shot that might bring others, like Chantry and Gillis, to help him?

She slipped the silk kerchief from around her neck and tied a round, good-sized stone in one end of it.

Then she studied the position of the hornet's nest, swung the loaded kerchief around her head a couple of times, and let fly with all her strength at the hanging nest.

She heard a "Plop!" as the stone hit the nest and broke a good-sized chunk out of it. The chunk fell, with a cloud of angry insects around it, and Annie, ducking out of sight, grinned to herself as she heard the lookout's anguished yells. She peeked out and saw him jumping about, waving his arms and trying to beat off the bad-tempered attackers.

Then, with a final howl of pain, he grabbed up his rifle,

jumped down from one boulder to the next, and finally, still fighting off his attackers, disappeared up the trail.

She could hear his yells dying in the distance.

A few minutes later she and Tagg passed the lookout point safely. And then, turning a corner of the trail, they came suddenly in sight of the place she had heard of but had never expected to see: the notorious Halfway House, supposed to be both a fortress and a boarding house for outlaws and gunmen from all over the Territory.

There were several horses in the corral, and the sound of men's voices came from the open door. But there was no way for her to get close to it in the daylight, because it stood in the center of the clearing. She could only wait, in hiding, in the heavy, tangled thicket that nearly surrounded the clearing. After dark she could get close enough to size up the situation inside, she thought.

She told Tagg to watch the house, while she hastily led Target and Pixie off a hundred feet deeper into the pine woods and left them to nibble on the grass at the foot of the young trees. It was pale green and very lush, and she knew they wouldn't try to wander. But to make sure, she hitched both of them to sturdy mesquite bushes.

When she got back to Tagg, he told her excitedly, "I

just saw Miss Melinda and a funny-looking little old man wearing a dirty apron. He gave her a bucket and sent her around back of the house."

"Where is he now?" Annie asked quickly.

"He went inside again."

"I'm going to see if I can get close enough to talk to her. Don't show yourself. I'll be right back."

She took the rifle with her and started circling through the thick brush, fighting the thorny mesquite and the prickly cat's-claw acacia that barred her way.

In a few minutes, a little breathless and somewhat scratched, she came out behind the windowless rear of the house. Melinda was only a few yards away, struggling to crank a creaky windlass at a small well a dozen feet from the back of the house.

The effort was almost too much for her frail strength, and she nearly let go the crank a couple of times. At last she had the bucket up to the edge of the well, and lifted it to the ground safely.

As she bent to pick it up again, she heard Annie's low signal whistle. She straightened up, looking around wildly.

Annie stood up in the underbrush and motioned hurriedly to her to come over.

Melinda ran to her and threw her arms around Annie's neck. "Oh! I knew you'd come to help us!"

"Don't know how much help we'll be," Annie told her soberly. "There's just Tagg and me right now. But we'll get Uncle Luke and a posse, soon as we can! Tell me what's going on!"

Annie kept a sharp lookout toward the house as Melinda hurriedly told her. "This awful man they call Tex won't believe Blair's forgotten where his claim was!" Melinda concluded. "He says he knows how to *make* him remember! Oh, Annie! I'm so frightened! What can we do?"

"First, we'll get you away from here—" Annie broke off suddenly at the sound of footsteps coming around the side of the house. "Get out of sight, and don't move!" Then as Melinda obeyed and disappeared into the brush, Annie ran as fast as she could to the well and crouched down behind it, her rifle ready.

Cookie was worried. Tim Johnson had come running in, yelling with pain from a hundred hornet stings, and the others had laughed at him. It was Cookie who had remembered that mud took the pain out, and he had sent Melinda to bring him some extra water to make poultices for the unhappy guard.

When she hadn't returned with it after a reasonable time, he had decided to go look for her. Now, as he came in sight of the well, he saw the filled bucket—but no Melinda.

He was just reaching for the bucket when Annie rose suddenly from behind the well with a leveled rifle. "Up with your hands, mister, and don't make a sound!" she ordered in a stern whisper.

Cookie's hands flew up at once. He shook his head sadly. "I know who you are, ma'am. You're a bang-up shot with a rifle, but if you've got Miss Melinda hid out, the two of you better leave quick. There's four mean hombres in there that wouldn't mind blastin' you down on sight!"

"That sounds like friendly advice," Annie replied drily, "but how come you're on our side?"

"Made up my mind to that when I heard Tex Chantry shot your kid brother! Besides, Murdock's always treated me square—not like some people!"

Annie lowered her rifle. "All right. You can go back. I'll take a chance you won't send them trailin' us!"

"You can trust me, ma'am," he said solemnly, "only— get to movin'!"

He waited there till he heard Annie and Melinda moving

away rapidly through the brush. Then he picked up the bucket of water and started slowly back to the house, giving them as much time to get away as he dared.

At the last minute he rushed through the front door, giving a good imitation of anger as he reported that the girl had slipped away and he hadn't been able to find her. "She musta run into the woods, poor thing!"

Tex Chantry had been having a quiet talk with Deuce at one end of the long pine table. He looked up and laughed. "Let her go. She'll come creeping back as soon as it gets dark . . . unless she gets lost!"

Beside the fireplace, Blair Murdock had been staring despondently at them. When he heard Chantry's words, he jumped to his feet with an expression of alarm. "You can't let her wander around out there! The woods are full of wild animals!" He struggled with the ropes that tied his hands.

"Maybe I better go look for her," Cookie suggested weakly, hoping Tex would forbid it.

His hopes were realized. "Stay here and tend to your cooking," Chantry growled. "If she runs into a bear or a wildcat, that's her hard luck." He laughed cold-bloodedly and turned to Murdock. "Of course, if you'd like to go look for her before it gets dark and they start prowling, all you have to do is tell us first where you dug that ore!"

Murdock made a hopeless gesture and sat down. "I can't tell you because I don't remember," he said dully. "Can't you realize I'd be glad to, especially now?"

Chantry glared at him. "You remembered all the rest. You're bluffing, trying to keep the strike for yourself. But I'm calling your bluff right now."

He and Deuce both rose and started to strap on their gun belts. "Saddle up," he told Deuce, "and get him loaded on. And you, Gillis, buckle on a gun and come along. We got a job for you."

Sam Gillis fumbled nervously as he strapped a gun belt around his waist, and dropped a borrowed gun into its holster. "Where we goin', Tex?" he asked.

"You'll find out when we get there," Chantry snapped impatiently.

As Deuce and Gillis led the tall young prisoner out the door, Chantry turned abruptly to Cookie.

"Where's the hide of that deer you shot?"

Cookie blinked with surprise. "It's pegged out on the storeroom wall. I figger it'll make a good thick curtain for the bunk-room window when winter sets in."

"Fetch it here! I need some rawhide strips."

Cookie's eyes widened. He was beginning to suspect what Chantry had in mind. "But—what—?" he tried to delay the gambler. "It's still mighty green!"

"That's how I want it! Get it!"

And when Cookie had reluctantly brought the deerskin to him, Tex Chantry set to work cutting long thin strips from it, while Cookie watched uneasily and slapped mud poultices on Tim Johnson wherever he needed them and some places he didn't.

When Chantry had half a dozen long strips cut, he gathered them together and rose. "Where's that gun Deuce took from the Oakley girl?" he asked.

Cookie handed it over reluctantly, and Chantry struck it into his pocket and stalked out.

Annie had brought Melinda to where Tagg was waiting and watching the house. They stayed back in the underbrush, listening to the men's voices at the corral as they saddled up.

"I think you and Tagg had better get started down right off," Annie advised Melinda. "I'll stay and see what's going on. Go straight back to Diablo, and Uncle Luke."

But Melinda rebelled. "I can't leave Blair!" she said a

little hysterically. "Maybe if I go back to the house, I can help him!"

"They'd like that!" Annie said grimly. "They'd know your brother wouldn't dare try to escape if they had you as a hostage again!" She stopped abruptly, as they all heard hoofbeats. "Wait a minute! Some of them are riding away. Maybe they've gone to look for you!" She left them and pushed through the sharp-thorned bushes to get a look at the four men who were riding away from the corral.

She studied them with a puzzled frown as they rode away speedily into the pine woods. Then she came back to Melinda and Tagg and announced cheerfully, "No use going back now, anyhow! It looks like he's managed to remember! He just rode out with Chantry and Deuce and that worm, Sam Gillis!"

"Oh!" Melinda smiled in relief. "Maybe they'll let him go now! He promised me he'd let them have the gold strike free and clear, if he could only recollect where it was." She turned happily to Tagg. "Now we won't have to hurry back to Diablo. We can wait here till they return!"

Annie caught Tagg's eye and shook her head slightly, being careful not to let Melinda see her do it. "Tell you what!" she said brightly to Melinda. "It may be hours before they get back. His claim may be miles away. So you better let Tagg take you down to that cave we found, and you two can wait there comfortably."

Melinda reluctantly agreed, but before she and Tagg started, Annie maneuvered to get Tagg aside unnoticed and whisper to him, "Leave her there, and hit out fast for Diablo! I don't like the look of things. Murdock was trussed up and tied to his saddle, and Deuce Adams was riding close behind him with a gun in his hand!"

21   The End of a Crooked Trail

Sheriff Luke had tried desperately since early morning to find anyone in Diablo who had seen Annie and Tagg last night. He had failed completely.

The town was buzzing about Melinda Murdock not showing up to open school. Half of them thought she had eloped with the missing gambler, handsome Tex Chantry. But there were some who wondered if she had slyly snatched Sam Gillis from his dragon wife. Though why she would want him, no one could imagine!

Sheriff Luke, pacing his office floor, waited to hear from Annie. He was worried deeply, but he had confidence in her bravery and resourcefulness. He felt that Annie and Tagg must be trying to help Melinda and her brother, but he had no reason to connect the gambler and Gillis with their mysterious absence.

Tagg showed Melinda the small cave and made her as comfortable as possible. "I think I'll look around down the trail a way," he said matter-of-factly. "Annie'll be along as soon as she gets a chance to talk to your brother."

"I'll wait right here, out of the sun," Melinda assured him cheerfully. "Don't worry about me at all."

Tagg rode Pixie slowly down the trail until he was out of sight of the cave. Then he slapped the little pony with his hat and tried to make it hurry. But Pixie stubbornly refused to move at more than a leisurely jog trot, and though Tagg pleaded and cajoled, he finally had to give up and let the pony take his own sweet time on the desert crossing.

Up at Halfway House, Annie crouched in the thicket and waited, watching the front of the house. It had been an hour since the four men rode away. She wished that Cookie would come out again, so she could ask him where Murdock had been taken.

Then she heard riders on the woods trail, and a moment later she saw Tex Chantry and Deuce approaching. Deuce looked grim, but Chantry seemed in a jovial mood. There was no sign of the other two, Sam Gillis and young Murdock.

They left their saddled horses in the corral and went slowly into the house, apparently having some sort of disagreement as they entered.

Annie was still puzzling when Cookie came out, leading Tim Johnson by the arm. Johnson was roughly bandaged around the face and head, and his hands were bound in muddy-looking rags. Cookie led him toward the top of the trail, and Annie heard Johnson whine as they went by, "I'm pickin' up my things at the outpost right now, an' headin' north! This outfit's worse'n a nest of rattlers! Laughin' at a man that's sufferin'!"

"Yeah," Cookie agreed soothingly. "I'm pullin' out myself, soon as I can get packed. Good luck, pal!"

"So long, Cookie! See you in jail!" Johnson called back, as he plunged down the trail and disappeared.

Cookie looked after him. "One less," he said aloud, and then gave a little, low owl-hoot, which Annie promptly answered from close by in the brush.

Cookie made a quick motion with his hand toward the rear of the house, and started in that direction himself, casually sauntering, whistling carelessly.

When he was out of range of the narrow side windows, he ducked into the underbrush and met Annie.

"Where did they take Murdock?" she asked quickly.

He nodded toward the woods trail. "Out there somewhere. Gillis is with him."

"What's going on?" She could see that he had something unpleasant on his mind.

He took a quick look toward the house to see that no one had come looking for him; then he said bluntly, "They've got him in a gun-trap. If he don't tell Gillis pretty quick where he got that ore, he's a dead one!"

"A gun-trap? What's that?"

"Chantry rigged a gun to a tree with rawhide, and tied Murdock to another tree across from it. Sun dries the rawhide an' makes it shorten up fast. After a while it pulls back the trigger and—*boom!*"

"Oh!" Annie was horrified. "But Gillis won't let it go off, will he? That would be—murder!"

"He's got his orders. Murdock tells, or Gillis leaves him where he is!"

"How long . . . ?" Annie couldn't finish the question.

"No way of knowin'." Cookie shook his head. "Depends on how much sun hits that rawhide!"

"Thanks, Cookie." Annie had made up her mind to move. "Better get back before they come looking for you!"

"Good luck, Miss Oakley! And—better run! That hide dries fast!" He hurried back toward the house, while Annie started to cut over through the thicket to the pinewoods trail.

She had to fight her way through a thick tangle of thorns, but once she came into the woods trail she moved fast. And in a few minutes, when she heard voices up ahead, she was able to run soundlessly along the pine-needle-carpeted trail, her rifle ready for instant use.

Then she saw the two men. Blair Murdock, tied to a young pine tree, faced a Colt .45 fastened with narrow strips of rawhide to a sun-drenched tree trunk ten yards away. The nose of the six-shooter was pointed slightly downward, supported by a thong tied above. Another thong ran through the trigger guard.

Murdock was fighting the ropes that held him, his eyes fixed on the menacing gun. And Sam Gillis, fascinated and apparently horror-struck, watched from a distance.

While she was still many yards away, Annie saw the nose of the six-shooter move up. Now it was pointing at the lower part of Murdock's body. She knew that the thong that would pull the trigger must be shrinking just as fast as the upper one.

"Cut me loose!" Murdock called desperately to Gillis. But Gillis was so transfixed that he couldn't have moved even if he had tried to.

At any moment now the gun would be pointing at Murdock's heart. And when it did, the other rawhide thong would draw back the trigger and send the bullet speeding toward the helpless victim.

There was no time to run closer. Annie dropped to one knee, aimed quickly, and fired at the upper strip of rawhide.

The rawhide thong snapped apart as the bullet went through it, and the gun dropped heavily against the tree. Its weight pulled back the trigger and sent a bullet crashing into the ground at the foot of the tree.

Sam Gillis wheeled, saw Annie standing with the smoking rifle in her hand, and started to run. But Annie dropped a quick shot into the ground ahead of him, and he stumbled to a halt.

She gestured with her rifle as she strode up to him. "Get over there and untie those ropes!"

Sam Gillis, tripping over his own feet, scrambled to obey, his hands shaking so hard that he could scarcely open the knots he had helped to tie.

At Halfway House, Tex and Deuce were arguing bitterly. "I tell ya, I heard three shots!" Deuce snarled.

"And I say you're just jumpy! I bet Murdock's talking a blue streak to Sam right now, telling all he knows!"

"Three shots—fast!" Deuce insisted angrily. "I know what I heard, an' I'm layin' odds he got loose an' finished off Gillis!"

"Don't talk like a fool! I tied him too tight!"

"We oughta go back an' see if somethin's gone wrong!"

"What could go wrong?" Chantry was losing patience.

"Plenty of things!" It was Annie Oakley's voice, and she was standing in the doorway, wearing her own Colt .45 that they had left in the gun-trap. She moved in across the threshold and they saw that Murdock himself was following her, dragging a limp Sam Gillis along by his coat collar, and armed with Gillis' own gun.

Tex Chantry started to his feet, drawing his gun. But before it had more than cleared the holster, Annie had made a lightning-fast draw and had smashed it out of his hand with a bullet.

Through a cloud of smoke she ordered sharply, "Now both of you gents get your hands up while you're still able!"

And as they hastily obeyed, they heard Cookie laughing

behind them and calling out, "Good for you, Miss Oakley! I figgered you'd pull it off!"

A few hours later, when Tagg finally pushed his tired little pony into Diablo's main street, and tumbled out of the saddle into his uncle's arms, a strange cavalcade was already on its way across the last stretch of desert outside of Diablo.

And not long afterward, a shocked citizenry stared in amazement at the spectacle of Sam Gillis, the gambler Tex Chantry, and the fugitive outlaw Deuce Adams, riding single file ahead of Annie Oakley. They were roped to their horses, and their hands were tied behind them.

But most amazing sight of all was the schoolteacher Miss Melinda Murdock happily riding alongside the tall young man whom Diablo knew as "Bill Welton" the escaped outlaw. There were no ropes on Welton. Instead, he carried an efficient-looking six-shooter, and over his saddle there were three gun belts that obviously had belonged to the miserable-looking trio who were leading the strange parade.

It was said later that Mrs. Sam Gillis had fainted when she heard the news about Sam, but that didn't sound like her. All that anyone could say for sure was that the humiliated gossip put her hotel up for sale, and left town on the stage next day without saying good-by to anyone.

That same day, the Tumbleweed Wagon rolled into Diablo to pick up lawbreakers and take them to Bonanza City for trial. When it rolled out again, it took the captured trio, in leg irons. And Diablo was glad to see them leave.

But Sheriff Luke, after a long talk with the United States marshal in charge of the wagon, himself drove Blair Murdock over to Bonanza City, and Annie went along to testify for him.

It was a short trial. When the Judge had heard Murdock's story, he decided that the young man had not been legally to blame for anything he had done while he was not in his right mind and believed himself to be a hunted outlaw.

And a couple of days later, at the ranch, there was a happy reunion between Melinda and her brother.

"I'm almost sorry I won't be able to teach school here next term," Melinda told Annie later, "but I'm going to make a home for Blair when he gets the cabin built near our claim."

"Thought he didn't know where it was!" Tagg looked surprised. "How did he find it again?"

"Pixie found it! And you and I spent the night in it!" Annie laughed. "And when he and I stopped to pick up Melinda on our way down with the prisoners, he recognized it!"

"Golly! Things turn out funny, don't they?" Tagg shook his head.

"Not funny, Tagg. Pretty wonderful!" Melinda smiled. "Thanks to somebody I can reach out and touch right this minute!" And she laid her hand on Annie's and smiled affectionately at her.

And Uncle Luke, sitting apart from the younger ones, nodded to himself, and thought how empty the house had seemed without Annie and Tagg the other night, and how empty his whole life would be if they ever left. But all he said aloud was, "Now, Melinda! You're turning her head! And she's saucy enough now!"

And then they all laughed, and Annie tossed her braids and wrinkled her nose at him, as they settled down to a long happy evening in front of the fire.

CPSIA information can be obtained
at www.ICGtesting.com
Printed in the USA
BVHW040837070620
581005BV00011B/987